I0490305

ART BOOKS

FROM CRESCENT MOON PUBLISHING

Leonardo da Vinci
by James Pearson

Early Netherlandish Painting
by Rosalind Mutter

Piero della Francesca
by Naomi Haskell

Giovanni Bellini
by Julia Davis

Eric Gill: Nuptials of God
by Anthony Hoyland

Minimal Art and Artists In the 1960s and After
by Laura Garrard

Postwar Art
by George Knighton

Vincent van Gogh: Visionary Landscapes
by Stuart Morris

Max Beckmann
by Stuart Morris

Egon Schiele: Sex and Death in Purple Stockings
by D. Simon Eade

Mark Rothko: The Art of Transcendence
by Julia Davis

Jasper Johns
by L.M. Poole

Brice Marden
by Laura Garrard

Frank Stella: American Abstract Artist
by James Pearson

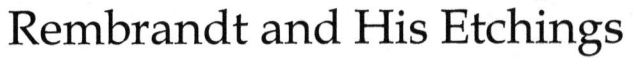

Rembrandt and His Etchings

Rembrandt and His Etchings

A Compact Record of the Artist's Life, his Work and his Time. With the Complete Chronological List of his Etchings Compiled by A. M. Hind, of the British Museum

Louis A. Holman

CRESCENT MOON

First published 1921. This edition © 2018.

Printed and bound in the U.S.A.
Set in Book Antiqua 10 on 14pt.
Designed by Radiance Graphics.

Thanks to the authors and publishers quoted.

British Library Cataloguing in Publication data

ISBN-13 9781861717177

CRESCENT MOON PUBLISHING
P.O. Box 1312, Maidstone, Kent, ME14 5XU
Great Britain, www.crmoon.com

Contents

NOTE ON THE TEXT

The text is from *Rembrandt and His Etchings* by Louis Holman, published by Charles E. Goodspeed & Co., Boston, MA, 1921.

The illustrations in the original text are included in the illustrations section, along with many other works.

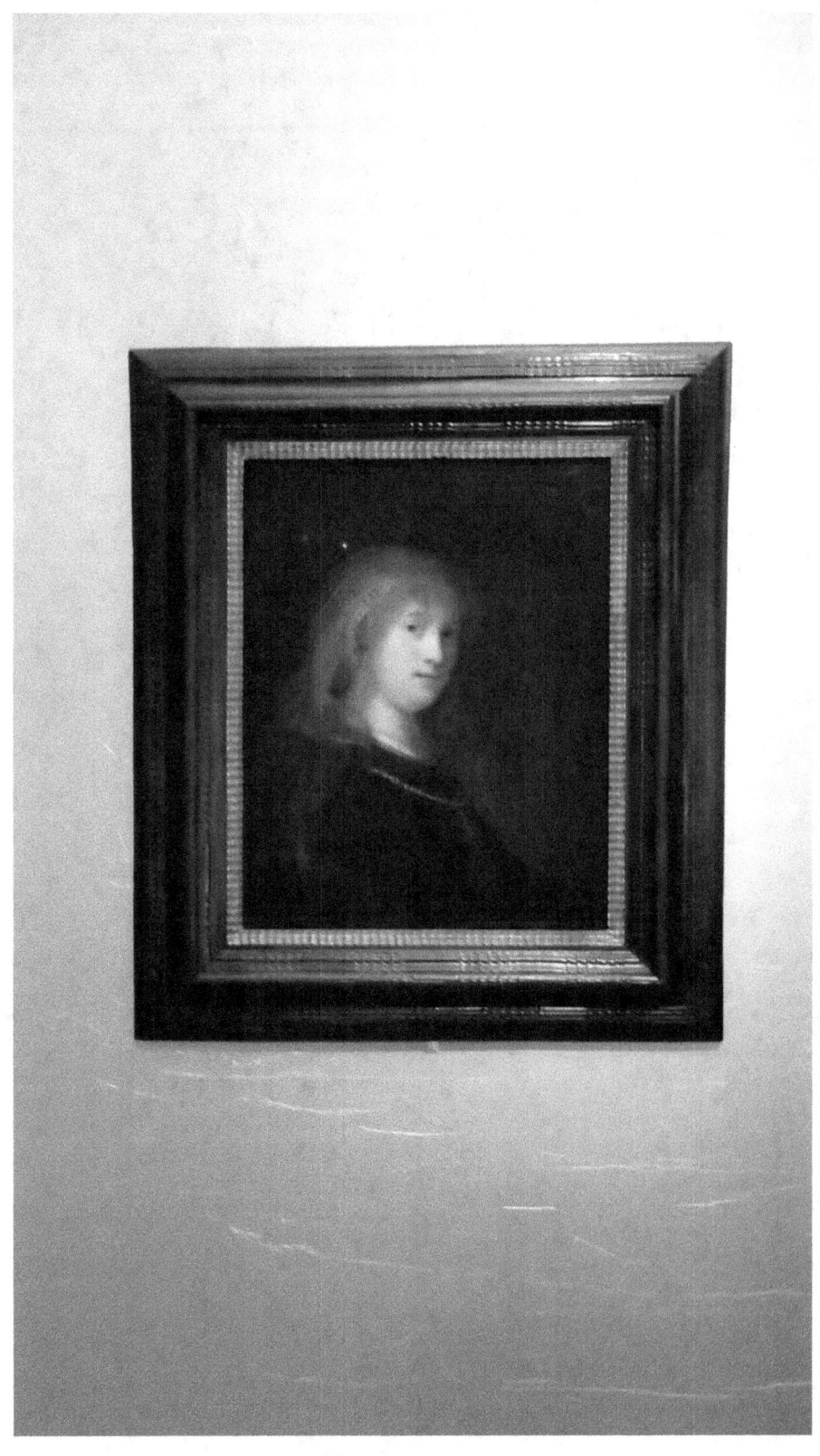

Rembrandt, Self-Portrait, Amsterdam

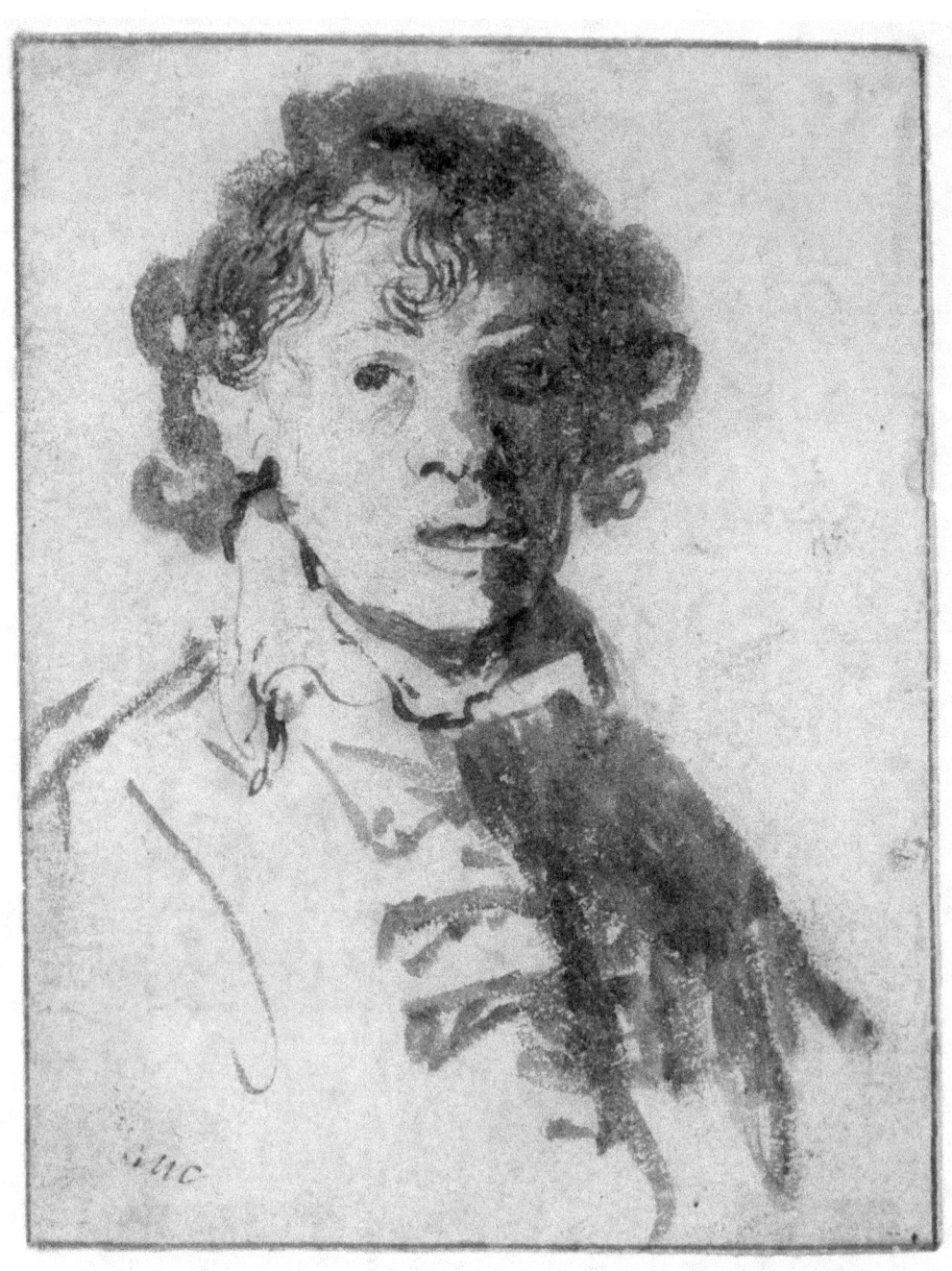

Rembrandt van Rijn, Self-Portrait With Open Mouth, 1629, British Museum

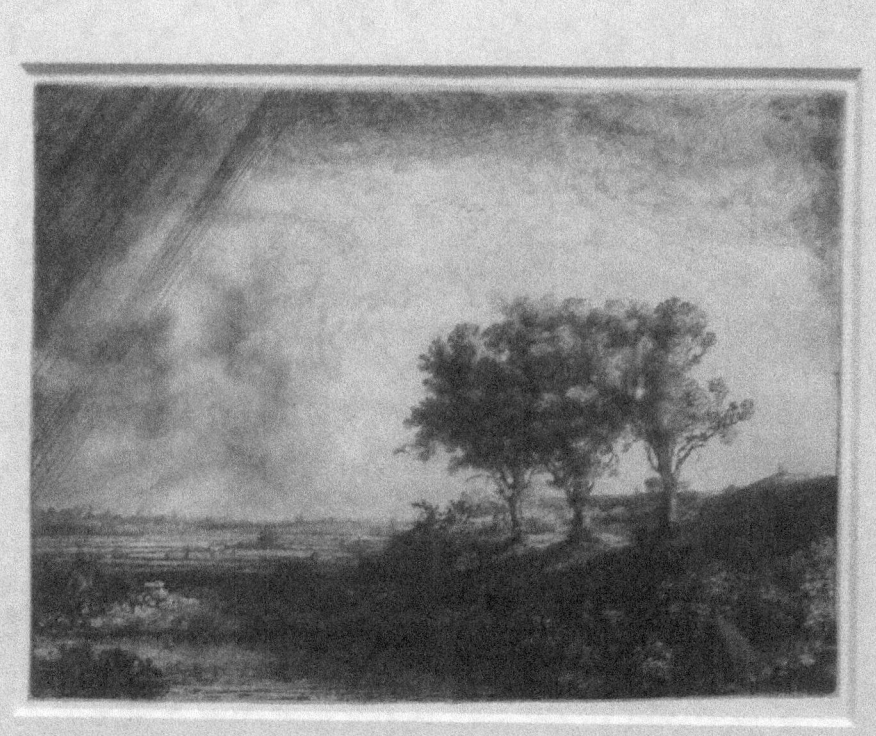

Rembrandt, Three Trees

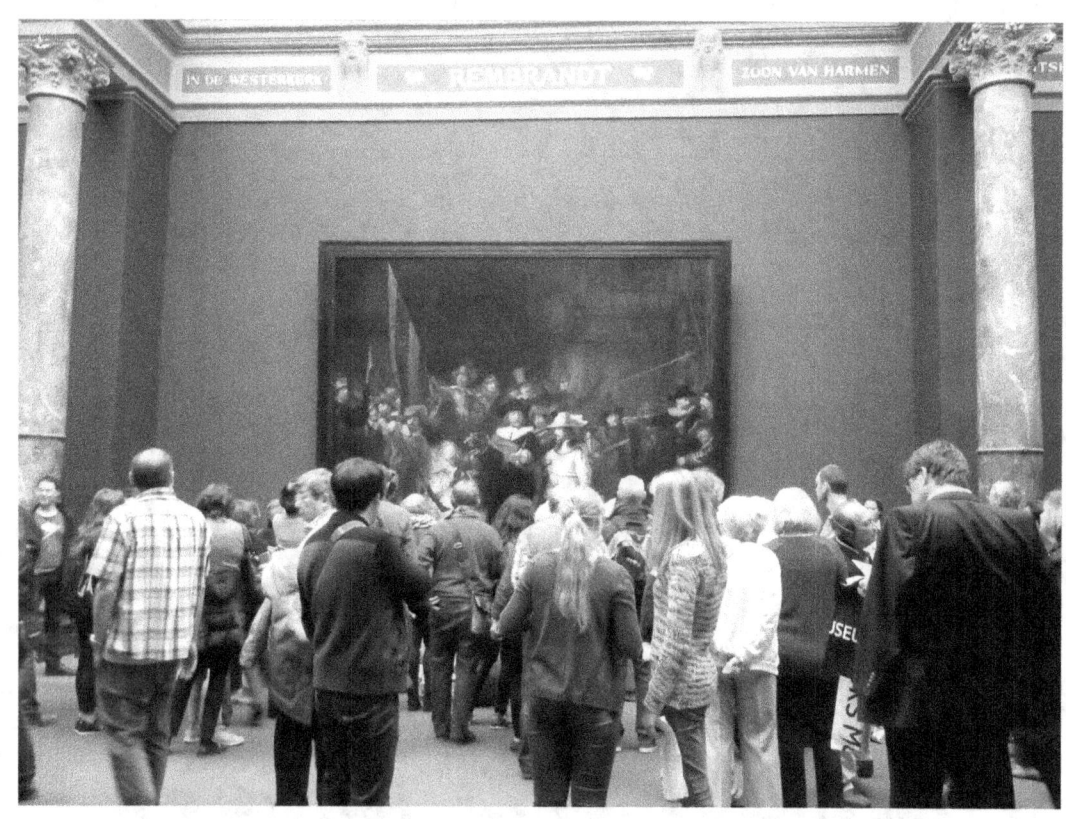

Rembrandt's Night Watch in the Rijksmuseum, Amsterdam
(photo: J. Robinson, 2015)

REMBRANDT AND
HIS ETCHINGS

"A fair & bewtiful citie, and of sweete situation" and famous for "ye universitie wherwith it is adorned;" such was Leyden as the fresh eyes of the youthful William Bradford saw it when the little company of English exiles, later revered as the Pilgrim Fathers, sought asylum in Holland. The fame of Leyden was to be further perpetuated, although Bradford knew it not, by one who had but just been born there when the English pilgrims came to the friendly university town; one who has added to the fame of his native place chiefly because he did not attend that university, which seemed so attractive to young Bradford. The father of this boy determined that he should have a collegiate education that he might sometime hold a town office, and fondly hoped that he was preparing him for it (in, perhaps, the very schools attended by the English children), when the lad made it clear to all men that he had no head for Latin and a very decided talent for drawing. So it came to pass that at the time Bradford and his friends set their faces toward America, and per-force turned their backs upon that "goodly & pleasante citie which had been ther resting place near twelve years," Rembrandt Harmens van Rijn, the youngest son of a miller of Leyden, turned his face, too, from the old toward the new. They sought liberty to live and to worship according to the bright light in their hearts: he, too, sought liberty to follow in a no less divinely appointed path, impelled thereto by an irresistible force which, after half a century, retained all its early vigor. They broke from the ways of their fathers and bore an important part in the development of the great American nation; he emancipated himself and his art from the thraldom of tradition and conventionality and became the first of the great modern masters of art.

The twelve-years' truce between the humiliated Dons and the stocky Dutchmen was now nearing its end, and Bradford says, "There was nothing but beating of drumes, and preparing for warr." This was one of the reasons why the peaceable Pilgrims sought a new home beyond the sea. But Rembrandt, already absorbed in his art-studies, saw nothing, heard nothing of these preparations; his ears were deaf to the drum-beats, his eyes were seeing better things than the "pride, pomp and circumstances of glorious war". There can be no question about his utter lack of interest in things military. When, at long intervals, he tried war-subjects (as most men sooner or later try their hand at the thing they are least fitted for) he failed pitifully. He could create a masterpiece of a "Man in Armor," or a "Night Watch," where the problems were purely artistic, and swords and flags were simply bits of fine color, but the painting or etching that breathed the actual spirit of war he could not produce. There is matter here for rejoicing. War and her heroes have had their full quota of the great artists to exalt their work. And now comes one who loved the paths of peace. With brush and etching-needle he made record for all time of the dignity and rare beauty which he found in ordinary hum-drum walks of life. We may even say that he exalted doctors and artists, housemaids and shopkeepers, yea even the very street-beggars, into such important personages that their portraits are still eagerly sought after by the great ones of the earth. It was during the lifetime of Rembrandt (1606-1669) that much of the wonderful development of Holland took place. She had come to her greatness gradually, but by the middle of the seventeenth century she occupied a leading place among the independent nations of Europe. Great discoverers, like Henry Hudson, had given her new dominions east and west, and colonization had begun. On the sea her flag was supreme; her merchant marine, going to and from her own possessions was seen in every port of the world; her admirals, Ruyter and Tromp, had won her an illustrious place forever in the annals of naval warfare. These were the days of Milton and Ben Jonson; of Cromwell, Gustavus Adolphus and Richelieu; of Murillo, Rubens and Van Dyck – days when Holland had within her own borders such men as Barneveld, the great statesman; Grotius, the father of international law; Spinoza, the philosopher and John de Witt, the Grand Pensioner – besides that noble group of artists: Hals, Cuyp, Ruysdael, Potter, Steen and Ostade. These days, too, saw the settling of many states in America, the founding of Quebec, New York and Boston.

Strangely apart from all these history-making movements, and from his peers among men, dwelt Rembrandt, the great master, in Amsterdam, serenely happy to-day in painting a portrait of his loved Saskia, to-morrow in etching the features of a wandering Jew. He had given himself, body and soul, to his art, and no man or movement of men could distract him from his work. Year by year his busy brain and dexterous hand produced paintings, etchings, drawings, in slightly varying proportion, but always in amazing quantity. For his forty-one productive years we find to his credit the average annual output of thirteen paintings, nine etchings, and thirty-nine drawings. And these numbers would be materially greater, doubtless, had we a full record of his work.

A few decades ago the ordinary person thought of Rembrandt only as a great painter; that time has fortunately passed. Modern engraving methods have made it possible to spread broadcast reproductions of his etched work. Thanks to these mechanical engraving-processes some of Rembrandt's etchings are now familiarly known and, to a degree at least, they are appreciated. No reproduction, however, can ever give the subtle quality of the original, and a revelation comes to one who looks for the first time on some brilliant, early impressions of his famous plates. The ink is still alive; the Chinese or Japanese paper which Rembrandt generally used, has sometimes gone very yellow and spotted, but oftener it has the fine mellowness of age. We treat it with respect, almost with reverence, for we recall that these very sheets of paper were dampened and laid upon the etched plate, already prepared by the hands of the great etcher himself. Each impression he pulled was as carefully considered as the biting of the copper plate. He varied the strength of the ink, the method of wiping, the pressure used; knowing the possibilities of his plate, he so manipulated it that it responded to his touch as a piano responds to the touch of a musician. The poor impressions and very late states, of which, unfortunately, many exist, are generally the work of those mercenary ones into whose hands the plates fell after his death – sometimes even before. Like a man with no music in his soul attempting to improve upon a sonata by Beethoven, these people not only printed, haphazard, poor impressions having the master's name, but sometimes even undertook to rearrange the composition and often to rework the plate.

No. 1. Rembrandt's Mother.

A hundred years before Rembrandt's time acid had been used to help out the graver. Durer, among others, used it, and he employed also, but in hesitating manner, the dry-point with its accompanying burr. Rembrandt's method of utilizing the roughness thrown up on the copper by the dry-point needle was a development of its possibilities that no one else, even among his own pupils, has ever equaled. It was much the same with everything else: the burin of the professional engraver he handled so skilfully that it is impossible to tell where the acid or the dry-point work stopped and the reinforcing work of the graver began. When others tried to combine these methods they failed. The hand of Rembrandt was the obedient servant of his mastermind: so well trained was it that with a preliminary sketch or without it, the needle produced on the smoked wax surface of the copper the picture which floated before him, so correctly that the brain was not diverted from the ideal picture by any crudity in the lines. If the tools, methods, and effects which the great engravers had used suggested anything to him, he freely took them up and bent them to his will. Making free use of all, binding himself to none, he always remained the versatile, independent student. And the strangest thing about it all is that he appears to have recognized, grappled with, and forever solved the problems of the art while nothing but a youth. One of the two etchings which bear the earliest date (1628) and signature is known as "Rembrandt's Mother: Head and Bust" (No. 1.) It is a delightful little plate, drawn with all the skill and freedom of a practiced hand. Frederick Wedmore, an English authority on etching says that "nothing in Rembrandt's work is more exhaustive or more subtle," and S. R. Koehler, an American authority, called it "a magnificent little portrait, complete artistically and technically," and very truly refers to it as "a prefiguration of what was to come." A man of twenty-two years already a master-etcher!

No. 210. Omval.

This etching measures just about two and a half inches square. There are others about the size of a postage-stamp, while the largest one, "The Descent from the Cross" (No. 103), is twenty-two by sixteen and a half inches. The amount of labor on these large plates is overpowering, while the workmanship in the smaller ones is almost unbelievably fine – think of a child's face not over one-eighth of an inch wide, and hands less than a sixteenth of an inch across, yet really eloquent with expression!

Rembrandt accepted the assistance of his pupils, as who among the old masters did not? He was, however, not practical enough to profit much by them: he could work to much better advantage alone. Among his thirty or forty pupils Ferdinand Bol, who came to his studio when only sixteen and stayed for eight years, gave his master most assistance. Bol's rendering is at times very much like Rembrandt's. Some critics think, for instance, that he etched most of the "Goldweigher" (No. 167) and "Abraham Caressing Isaac" (No. 148); both, however, are signed by Rembrandt. When these pupils established studios of their own, they made free use of their old master's compositions, subjects and figures.

With Jan Lievens, his fellow student at Lastman's studio, with van Vliet, Roddermondt and other engravers and etchers of the time, Rembrandt was on terms of great intimacy. They appear often to have worked on the same plate, and to have borrowed each other's ideas "without let or hindrance." Indeed, it is hard to comprehend the extent to which exchange of ideas was carried at that time. Here is a good illustration of the way things went without protest of any sort being raised. Hercules Seghers etched a large landscape with small figures, after a painting by Adam Elzheimer and an engraving by Count de Goudt, entitled "Tobias and the Angel." This copper plate came into Rembrandt's possession; he burnished out Tobias and his companion, and replaced them by Joseph, Mary and the Holy Child (No. 266). To cover the erasure he added foliage, but the wing of the angel, the outlines of a leg and various other unused portions of Tobias can still be seen. Rembrandt's reason for bothering with this plate is incomprehensible. He improved it, undoubtedly, but the composite result is exceedingly commonplace and reflects no credit upon any one. John Burnet, the etcher-author, has drawn attention to the fact that the figure of Christ in "Christ at Emmaus" (No. 282) is taken from one by Raphael, who is known to have borrowed it from da Vinci, and it is thought da Vinci, in his turn, got it from a former master. Rembrandt borrowed also from Rubens, Titian, Mantegna, his pupil Gerard Dou, Van de Velde and others. Many of his contemporaries and successors extended toward him the same sort of flattery.

More than half the subjects of Rembrandt's etchings are portraits and studies of the human figure; about one-quarter are scriptural or religious. There are two dozen landscapes, and the remainder are allegorical and fancy compositions. We find then the two most productive sources of his inspiration were the men of his day and the men of the Bible. This book appears to have been the only one he knew at all well, but of it he made excellent use. Despite the incongruities of his Biblical compositions, despite the broad Dutch features, the modern, gorgeous apparel and side-whiskers of the patriarchs, the pugilistic proportions of his angels, his etchings have a truth and vital force that there is no withstanding. Perhaps the very fact that he clothed his people in a fashion that he knew well made his pictures the more successful in reaching the hearts of men. In the all too realistic "Abraham's Sacrifice" (No. 283), in "Joseph's Coat Brought to Jacob" (No. 104), in the naive "Rest on the Flight" (No. 216), and many, many others, the story-telling quality is exceeding strong and the artistic work above criticism. When we look at "David in Prayer" (No. 258), beside his incongruous four-post bedstead, we cannot but feel that here penitence and sincerity is forcefully depicted. The acme of Rembrandt's religious work was reached, however in "Christ, with the Sick Around Him" (No. 236) (etched about 1650), which is often called the finest piece of etched work that has ever been produced. It is a combination of pure etching and dry-point, and in the second state, there is an India-ink wash in the background. There are, I think, nine copies of the first state extant; the last one sold at public auction (Christie's, 1893) brought over $8,500. While the Christ here is not so satisfying as the one in "Christ Preaching" (No. 256) which is remarkably strong and noble, it is Rembrandt's typical conception of our Lord – always ministering to real flesh and blood, the poor, suffering, common people. What a striking contrast with the resplendent artificiality which surrounds the Christ of the Italian masters.

No. 290. Jan Lutma, Goldsmith and Sculptor.

Rembrandt was his own most frequent model. He painted about sixty portraits of himself, and among his etchings we find about two score more. Some of them are large and finished, as the deservedly popular "Rembrandt Leaning on a Stone Sill" (No. 168), which is a perfect example of the possibilities of the etching-needle; others are mere thumb-nail sketches of various expressions of face. He used his mother many times, and also his wife and son. In all these is apparent a delightful sense of joy in his work. Nor is this desirable quality lacking in the wonderful series of large portraits of his friends: the doctors, the ministers, the tradesmen of Amsterdam. Perhaps these were pot-boilers, as some students of his work say, but surely never artist before or since produced to order a group of etchings that, taken entirely apart from his other plates would assure their author a high place among the greatest etchers. In the whole lot there are few that some authority on etching or some great artist has not held up as an example of work that even the master himself never surpassed. But an artist cannot always keep himself at concert pitch and when Rembrandt etched the portrait of his friend "Abraham Francen" (No. 291) I feel that he struck an uncertain, almost false note, unworthy of himself. We might, perhaps, account for this by saying, that it was done in 1656, the year of his bankruptcy were it not that the noble "Jan Lutma" (No. 290) which competes with the "Jan Six" (No. 228) for the place of masterpiece of the entire series, was made the same year. But he was an unaccountable sort of man who could produce in a poor, naked studio, with untold trouble stalking him on all sides, such an etching as the "Lutma," such a painting as the "Syndics of the Draper's Guild," both of which rank with the best products of his happy, care-free years of luxury.

It is noticeable that Rembrandt had no sittings from persons of high rank. So far as I can find "Burgomaster" is the most exalted title that can with certainty be given to any of his patrons. The reason is not far to seek. Rembrandt was not a courtier like Van

Dyck and Rubens; he was too independent and too busy to spend time kow-towing to society. A contemporary says of him, "When he painted he would not have given audience to the greatest monarch on earth." He calmly set at nought established principles and conventional rules, in etiquette as well as in art, and followed the bent of his genius with absolute disregard for the opinions of his fellows. The story of "Night Watch" is characteristic of Rembrandt and shows the whole situation in minature. The members of Captain Banning Cocq's Company of the Civic Guards were flattered by the offer of Rembrandt, then at the height of his fame, to paint their portraits. The sixteen members destined to figure in the picture gladly subscribed one hundred florins each, and great were their expectations; but even greater their disappointment when the picture was placed on view. All but a half-dozen felt that they had a distinct grievance against the painter. Had they not paid for portraits of themselves? And they got – what? Here a face in deep shadow, here one half-hid by the one in front, here one so freely drawn as to be unrecognizable. The artist had made a picture, to be sure – but their portraits! Where were their portraits – the portraits they had paid for? Rembrandt had thought out every inch of his picture: he was sure it could not be better, and change it he would not. The resentment was bitter and deep, and the Civic Guards in future bestowed their favors elsewhere.

There were, however, some fellow citizens who recognized his genius and sincerity. These stood by him. Samuel Manasseh ben Israel, whom Cromwell honored, was his neighbor on the Breedstraat, and an intimate friend. Then there were Jan Sylvius and Cornells Anslo, the Protestant ministers; Fan Asselyn and Clement de Jonghe, who were artists; Bonus and Linden, the physicians; Lutma, the goldsmith, and young Jan Six, "Lover of science, art and virtue." These and a few others are known and honored to-day chiefly because they were Rembrandt's friends. His recognition of their faithfulness to him was shown in a much more permanent form than they knew. Good impressions of his etched portraits of these men are still to be seen. They are, like all his etchings, rapidly increasing in value. A "Jan Six" sold recently for over $14,000; an "Ephraim Bonus" (No. 226) for $9,000. To possess such a portrait of an ancestor is little short of a patent of nobility. The Six family of Amsterdam happily have not only Rembrandt's oil-portraits of the Sixes of his day, but also good impressions of the etching of the burgomaster, and even the plate itself – that famous dry-point plate, which the artist worked on for weeks, and which his critics have worked over ever since. Some of these critics hold that even Rembrandt should not have attempted such complete tonality in an etching, that Jan Six urged him to it, and that, in short, as an etching, it comes near to the failure line. Other critics believe that the artist's idea was to show the utmost extent to which the art could be carried, and that in so doing he produced a masterpiece. Middleton, for instance, thinks that "it is not possible to conceive a move beautiful and more perfect triumph of the etcher's art." Few, it is safe to say, can see a good impression of an early state of this portrait without being struck by its great originality and beauty, and upon closer study, I feel a fair-minded person will inevitably fall under the spell of the wonderfully drawn face and hands, the deep, transparent shadows, and the soft, tender light which envelopes the whole.

(No. 266). The Flight into Egypt.

Although Rembrandt had a few such cultivated friends as those mentioned above, it was said of him by a contemporary German painter that "his art suffered by his predilection for the society of the vulgar." It certainly would have been more profitable for Rembrandt if he had always portrayed people of position and wealth, but that his art suffered because he many times used beggers for models it would be impossible to show. An interesting series of tramps, peddlers and outcasts began with the beginning of his career as an etcher, and ended twenty years later with the production of one of his most popular plates, "Beggars Receiving Alms at the Door of a House," (No. 233) a very freely handled, splendidly composed etching, in which surprisingly few lines judiciously placed do the work usually allotted to double their number. A little plate of less than four square inches, entitled "The Quacksalver," (No. 139), strikes me as the masterpiece of this series. Although Van de Velde is supposed to have given Rembrandt the idea for his drawing, his genius made it his own in realism and movement, and in its beauties of line, color and texture. "An Old Woman Sleeping" (No. 129)), although scarcely to be included in this series, is another that has wonderful spontaneity. This is no posed model, but one who has actually fallen asleep over her book; Rembrandt sees her, and before her "forty winks" are over, she is immortalized, and probably she never knew it. About 1640 Rembrandt began etching landscapes. They are free and simple in composition and treatment and show even greater force and more suggestive power than those that he painted. Practically all of his two dozen landscape plates hold undisputed first rank. They always have and probably always will. In "Landscape with Trees, Farm-buildings and a Tower" (No. 244), the tower is "ruined" in the third state. A first state print at the Boston Museum of Fine Arts shows the tower in good preservation. One of these prints sold at auction not long ago for over $9,000. Another of the exceedingly satisfactory etchings in the series, one that has exercised a great influence on landscape etching all the world over, is "Omval" (No. 210). Its creator seemed fond of the fine old tree in this plate. He used it several times elsewhere. "Six's Bridge" (No. 209) which is almost pure outline, and the "Three Trees" (No. 205), with its great sweep of flat country, have a right to all the praise showered upon them. They, too, are masterpieces.

While Rembrandt's genius made itself manifest in his landscapes, it surely is absent from most of his animal drawings. We must remember that if he ever went outside of Holland it was for a few months to the east coast of England, and that the opportunity for studying any great variety of animals in either place was not great. His horses, asses, hogs, etc., improve as the years advance. The little dog with the collar of bells is well drawn. He, undoubtedly, was a member of the family.

No. 256. Christ Preaching.

It is an interesting fact, at a time when the illustrating of books and magazines is such an important art, to know that Rembrandt was offered and accepted some commissions to make illustrations for books. These attempts to give form to another's ideas were not successful – in one case it was such a failure as to leave it still uncertain what he intended to illustrate. Vosmaer, his great biographer, says that this print "The Ship of Fortune" (No. 106), pictures incidents in the life of St. Paul, while Michel, another biographer, thinks that it illustrates events which gather about Mark Anthony and the battle of Actium!

A score of men – Bartsch, Wilson, Blanc, Middleton, Rovinski, to mention a few – have at sundry times and in divers places compiled annotated catalogues of Rembrandt's etchings. They, and other students like Vosmaer, Haden, Hamerton and Michel, have given years to study and travel in connection with their books on Rembrandt. All lovers of etching appreciate this and are grateful. Nevertheless, it is amusing sometimes to compare their expert testimony. About 1633 somebody etched a "Good Samaritan." Several of these experts regretfully, but frankly, admit that Rembrandt is the guilty one. Others are sure that a pupil did the worst of the work; Haden says it is entirely the work of another hand; while yet another declares that of all Rembrandt's etchings this particular "Good Samaritan" (No. 101) is his favorite. Middleton, to give another instance, thinks that the thick lines from top to bottom, in the fourth state of the "Christ Crucified between Two Thieves," ("The Three Crosses") (No. 270) are not Rembrandt's work, for they serve "to obliterate, conceal and mar every excellence it had possessed." Haden, however, considers that the time of darkness is represented, and that this particular state is far the finest in effect. Much confusion arises from the fact that sometimes all the states of a plate under discussion are not known to each critic. The whole matter of states is a confusing one. The old idea was that Rembrandt produced various states in order to make more money. But it seems plain now that when Rembrandt changed a plate it was for much better reasons than the making of a few guilders. We know, for instance, that the "Jan Six" plate was changed twice to make needed corrections, and that the second state of the first portrait of his mother simply carries out the original design. On the other hand, it obviously could not have been Rembrandt who made the third state of the "Jan Lutma," with its hard, ruled lines and great unnecessary window.

If in the days of hardship, when his son, Titus, peddled his etchings from door to door, he could have foreseen the great army of admirers who three centuries later should outbid each other at auctions, and make war in print over his experimental plates, his failures and his trial-proofs – now often exalted into "states" – the very irony of the thing would surely have brought him genuine satisfaction and relaxation.

Rembrandt has said of himself that he would submit to the laws of Nature alone, and as he interpreted these to suit himself, he cannot be said to have painted, or etched, or done anything in accord with our interpretation of recognized or well-grounded laws. With him it was instinct, pure and simple, from youth to old age. He had no secret process of painting or etching; but he had an amazing genius for both.

One October day in 1669 an old man, lonely and forgotten, died in Amsterdam. They buried him in the Wester Kerk and, that he might not be confounded with some other old man, they wrote in the "Livre Mortuaire" of the Kerk, "Tuesday, 8th oct., 1669, rembrant van rijn, painter on the rozengraft, opposite the doolhof. leaves two children."

Of material things he left little; but the two children: Cornelia, his fifteen year old daughter, and Titia, the posthumous, infant child of Titus, would keep his name alive! Less than a score of years and the family record comes to an abrupt end. No one to-day may claim descent from Rembrandt, but his name has not perished from the earth, nor his influence abated among the sons of men. His name took on new life when he laid it aside; his influence strengthened when he ceased personally to exercise it. Who of us is not his grateful heir? Who does not now do loving reverence to this poor "painter on the rozengraft, opposite the doolhof?" He surely stands among the immortals, one of the foremost painters of all time, the greatest etcher that has yet appeared.

NOTE – The foregoing article was published a few years ago in *The Craftsman*. Of the many commendations received at that time we print but one:

"New York, Dec'r. 5, 1906. Dear Mr. Holman; *** I send you my special thanks for your article on the etchings of Rembrandt. I have read it carefully, and let me say plainly that I think is the best short treatise on this great subject which ever I have read. The knowledge of the subject as treated by many writers is so superficial – but yours is profound. You have evidently made a serious study of your subject. Yours very truly,"

(Signed) Frederick Keppel.

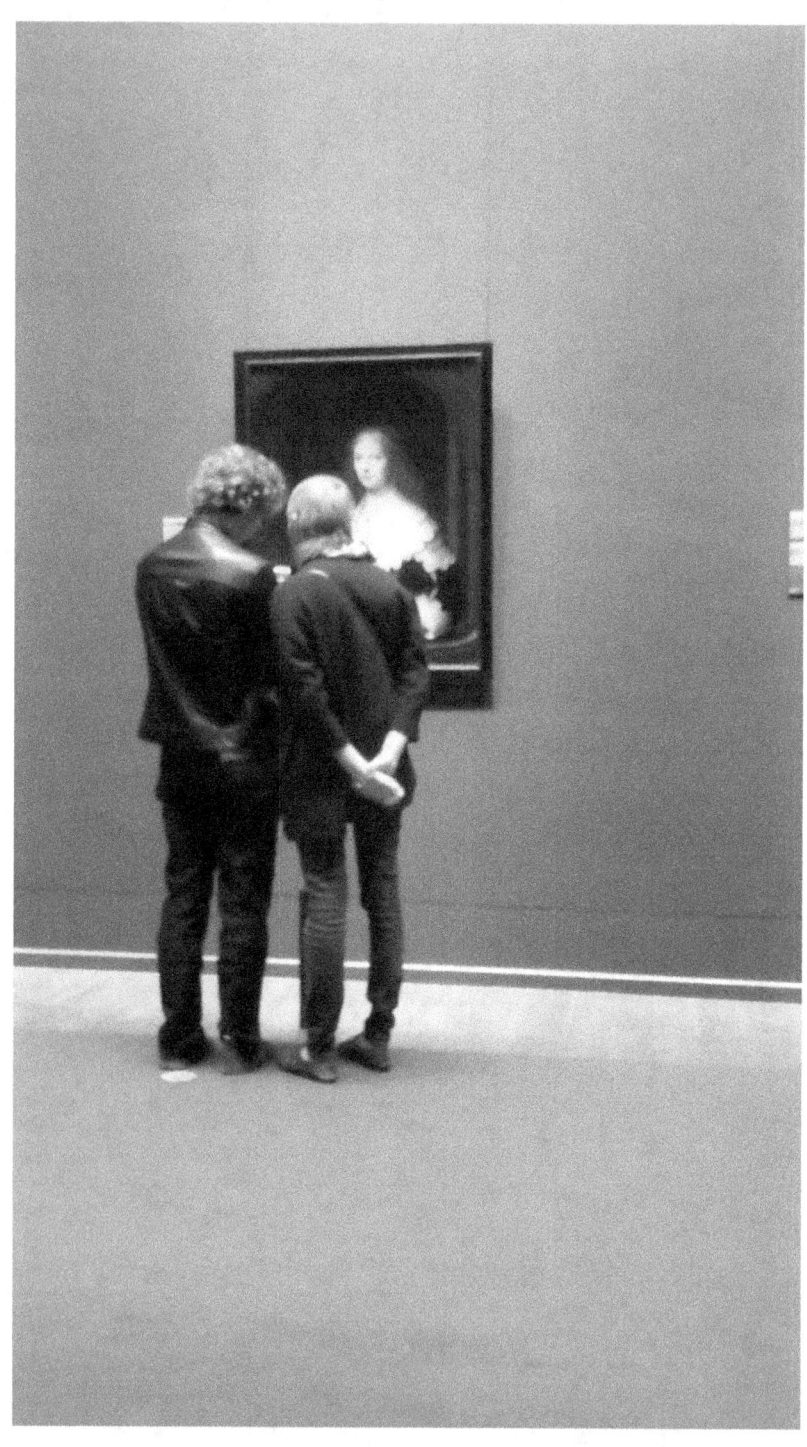

Rembrandt in the Rijksmusem, Amsterdam, 2015
(this page and over. Photos: J. Robinson).

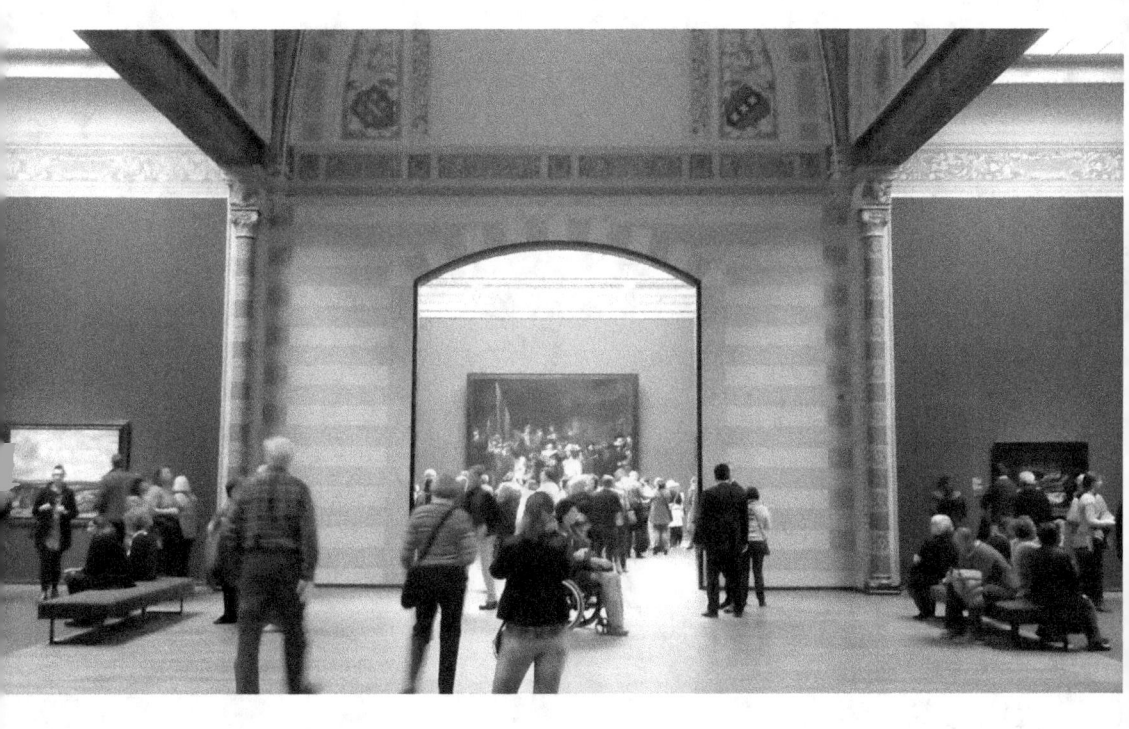

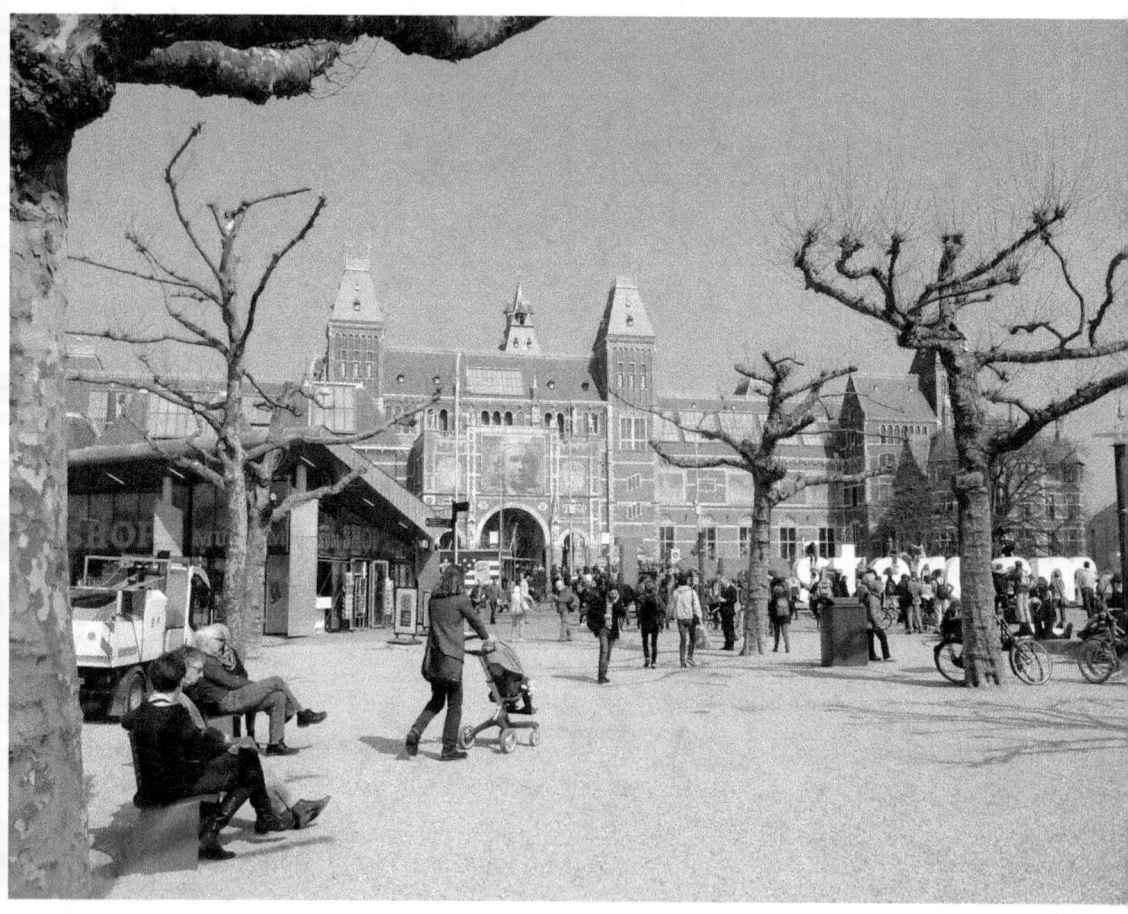

The Rijksmuseum in Amsterdam

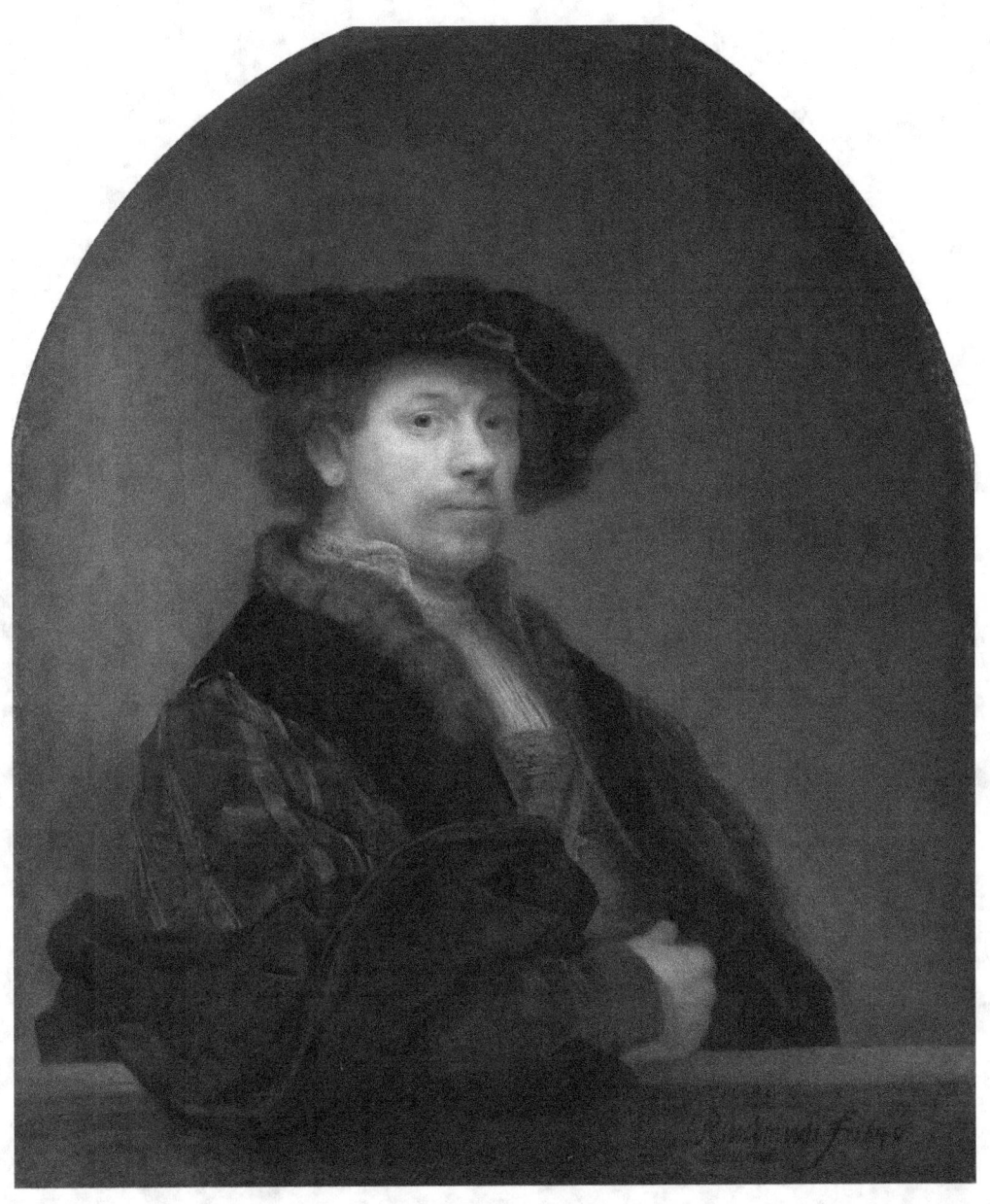

Rembrandt, Self-Portrait, 1640, London
(this page and over)

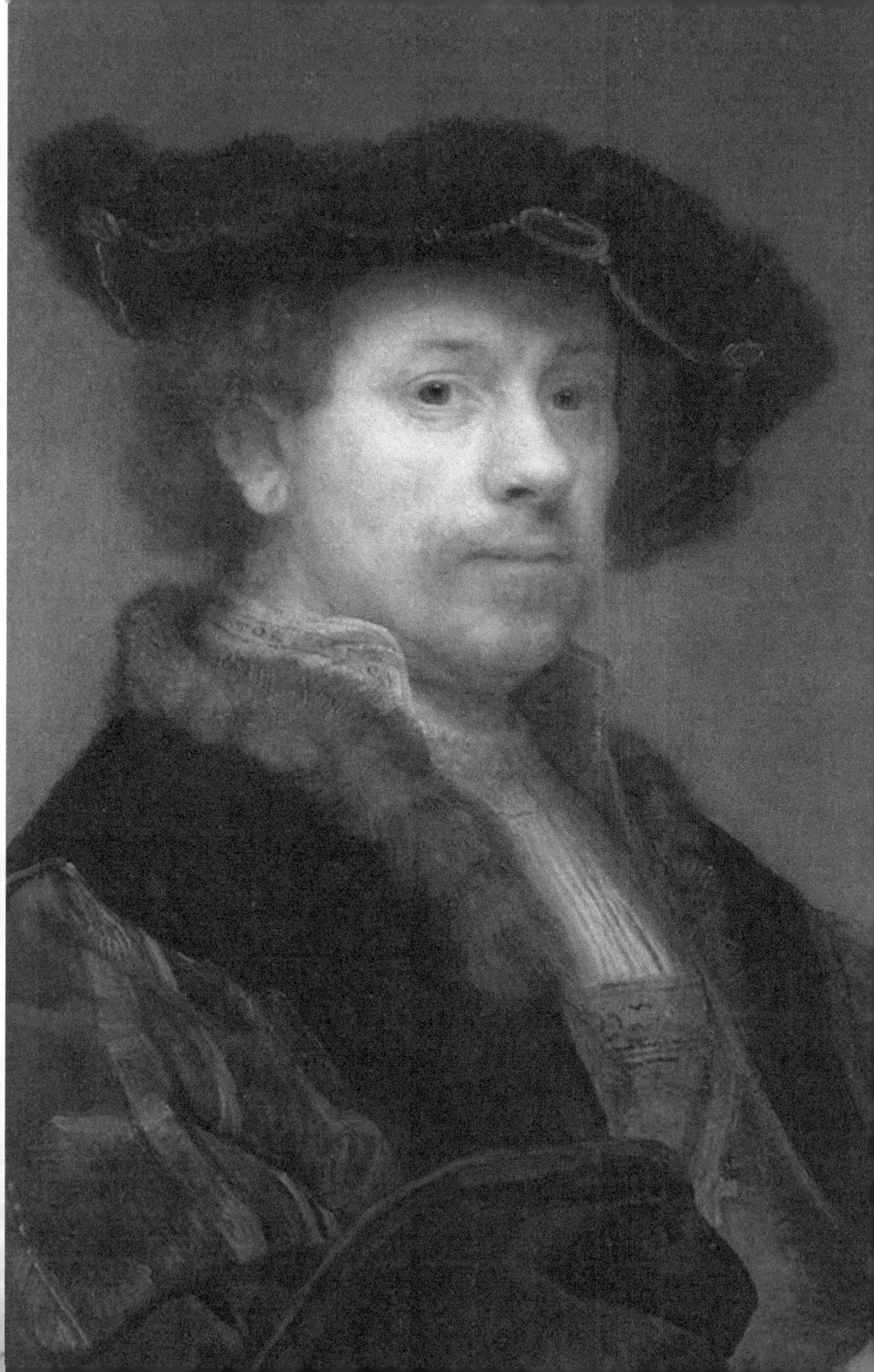

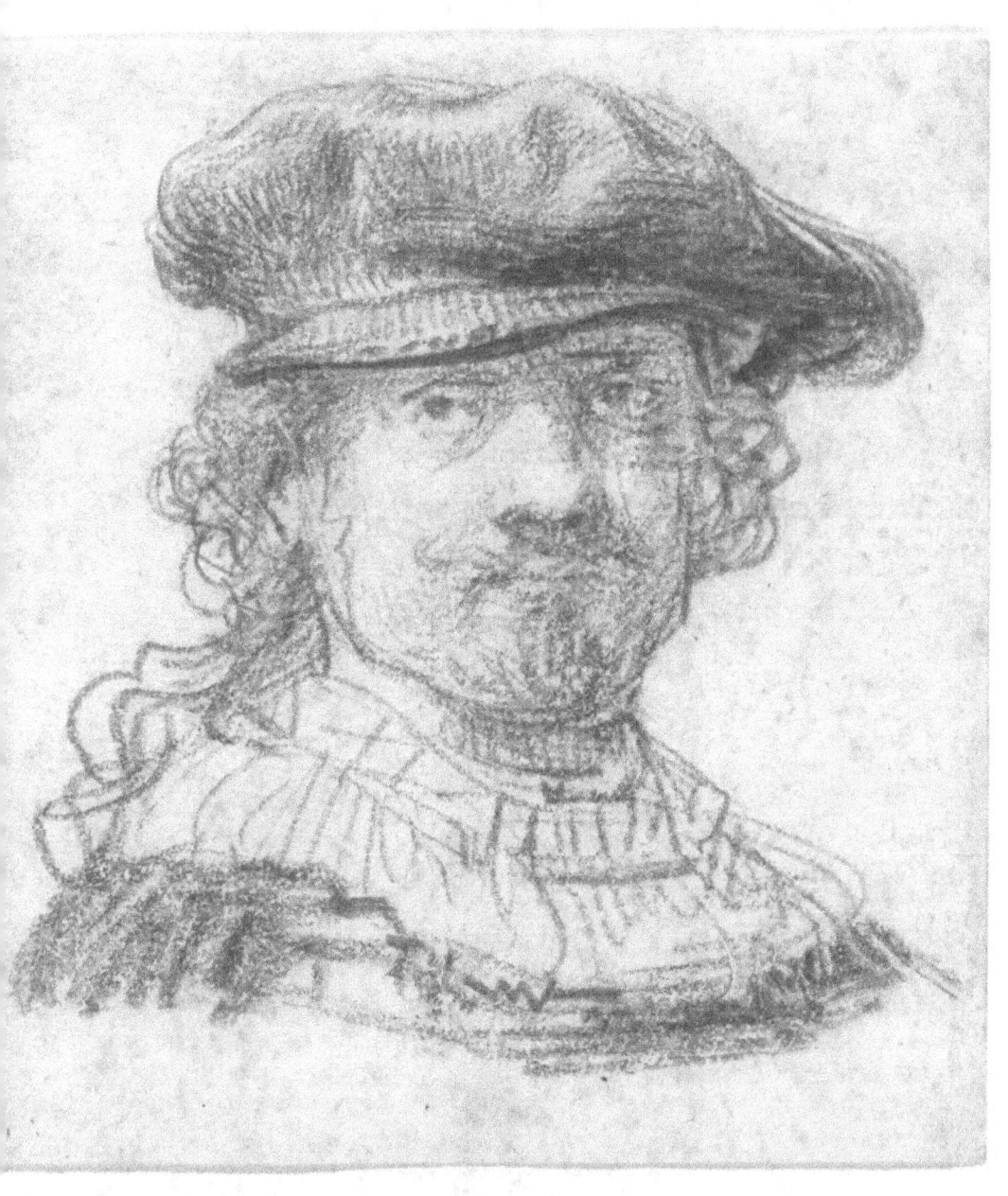

Rembrandt van Rijn, Self-Portrait, c.1637, Washington, DC

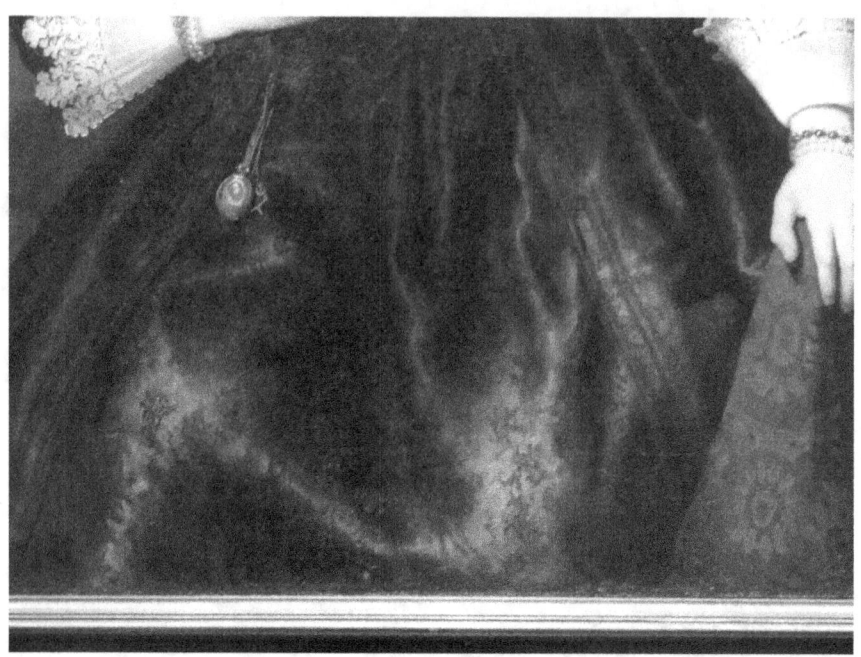

Rembrandt, Portrait of a Young Woman, details

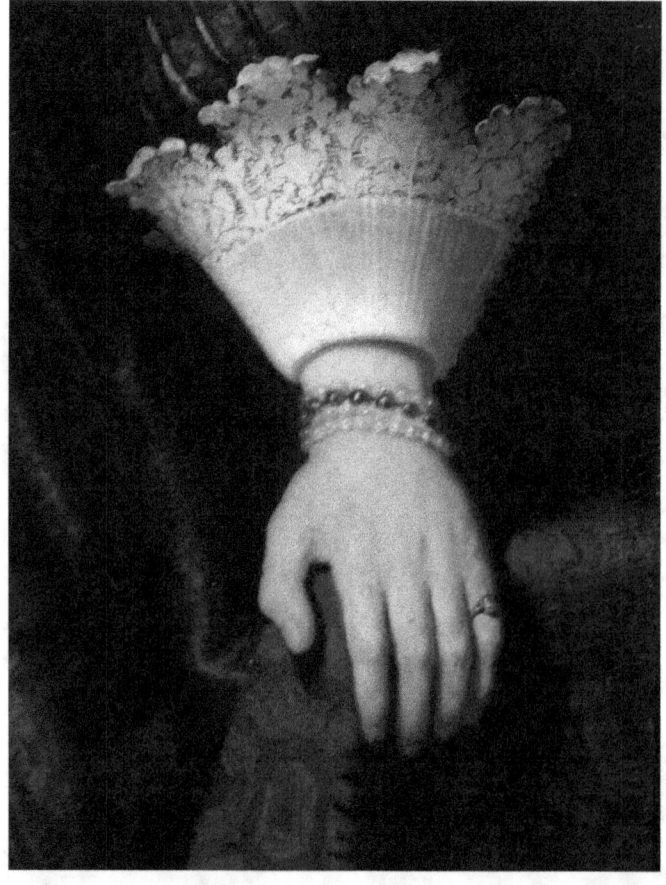

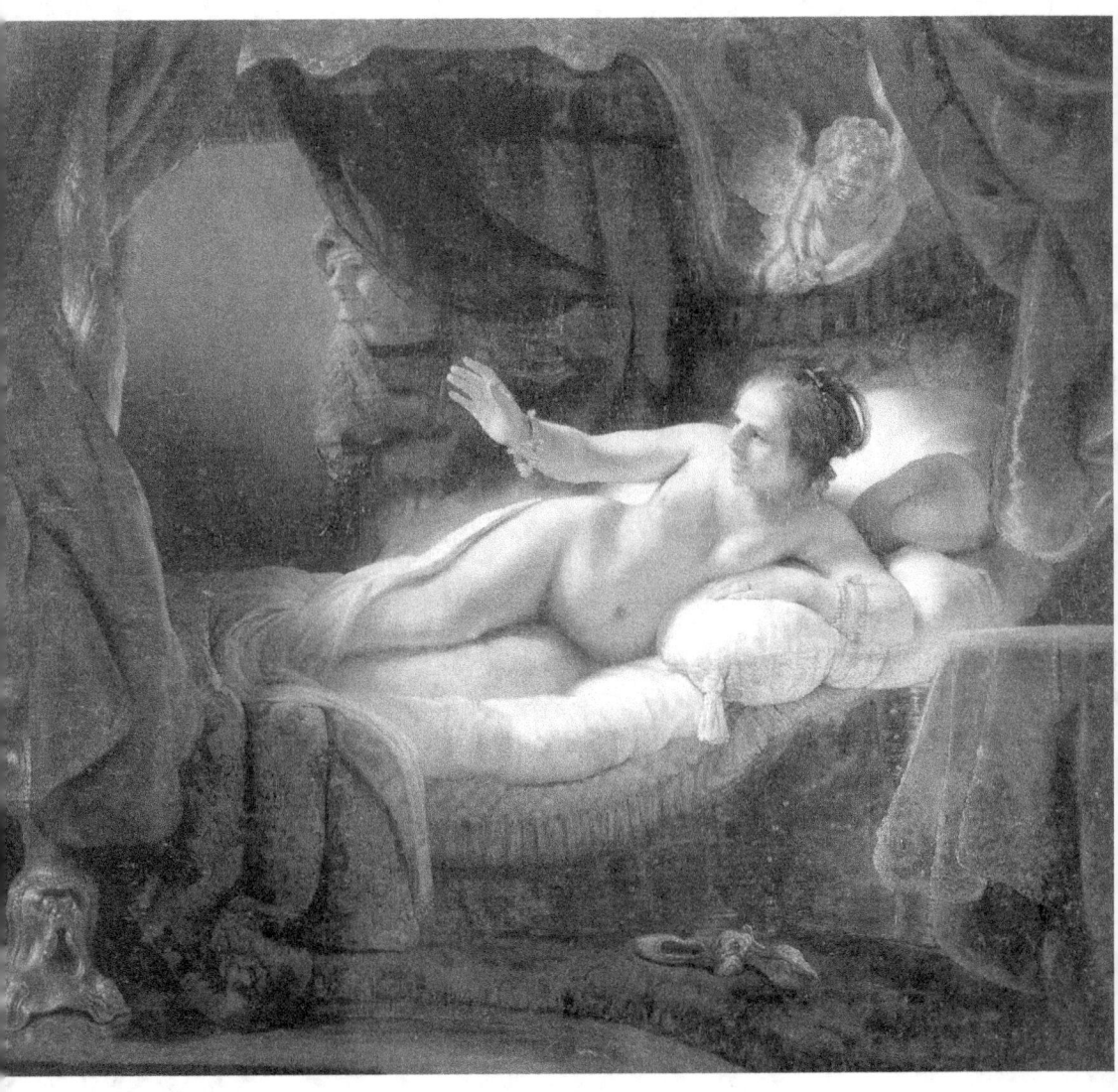

Rembrandt van Rijn, Danae, 1636, St Petersburg

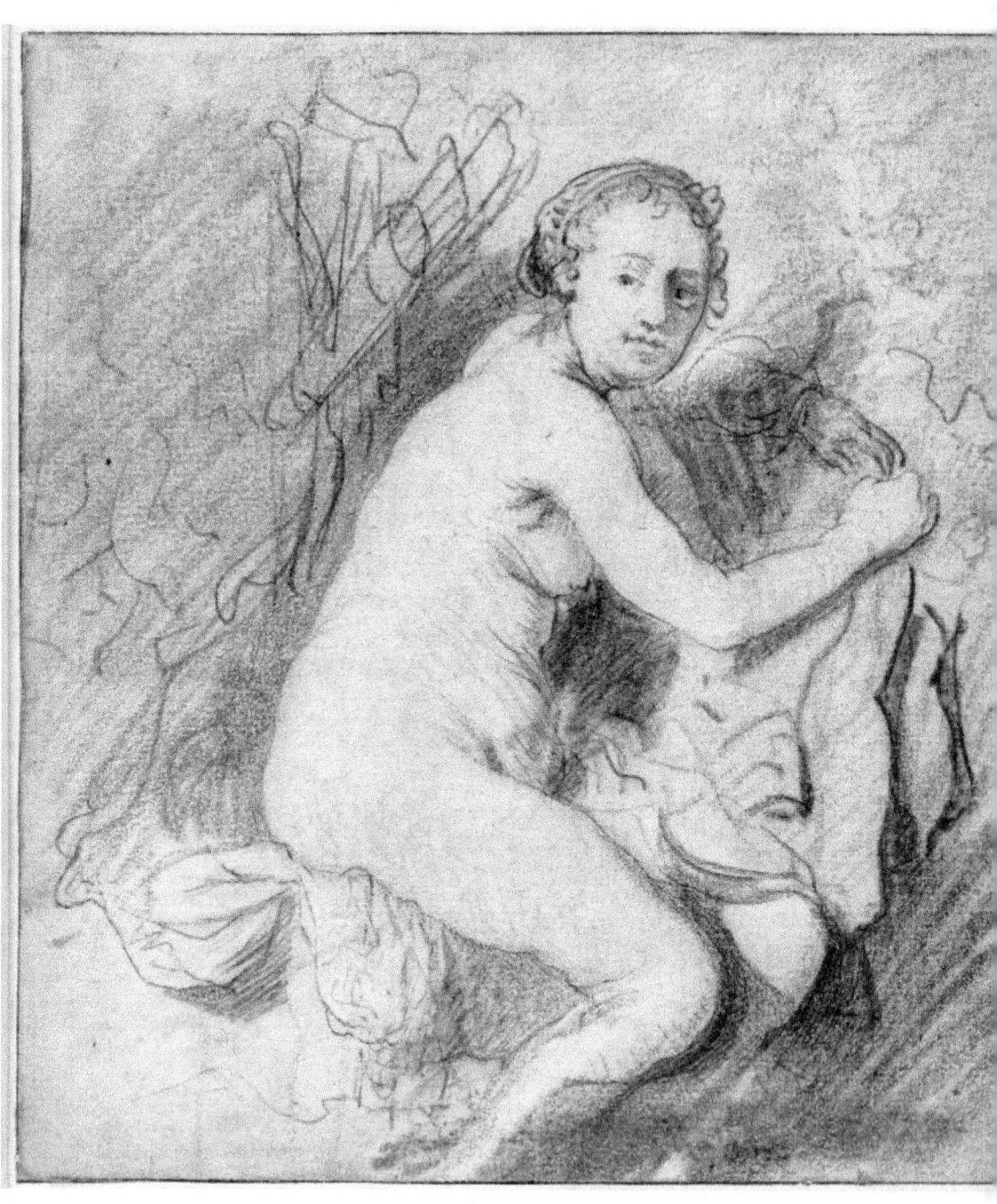

Rembrandt van Rijn, Diana At the Bath, 1630-31, British Museum

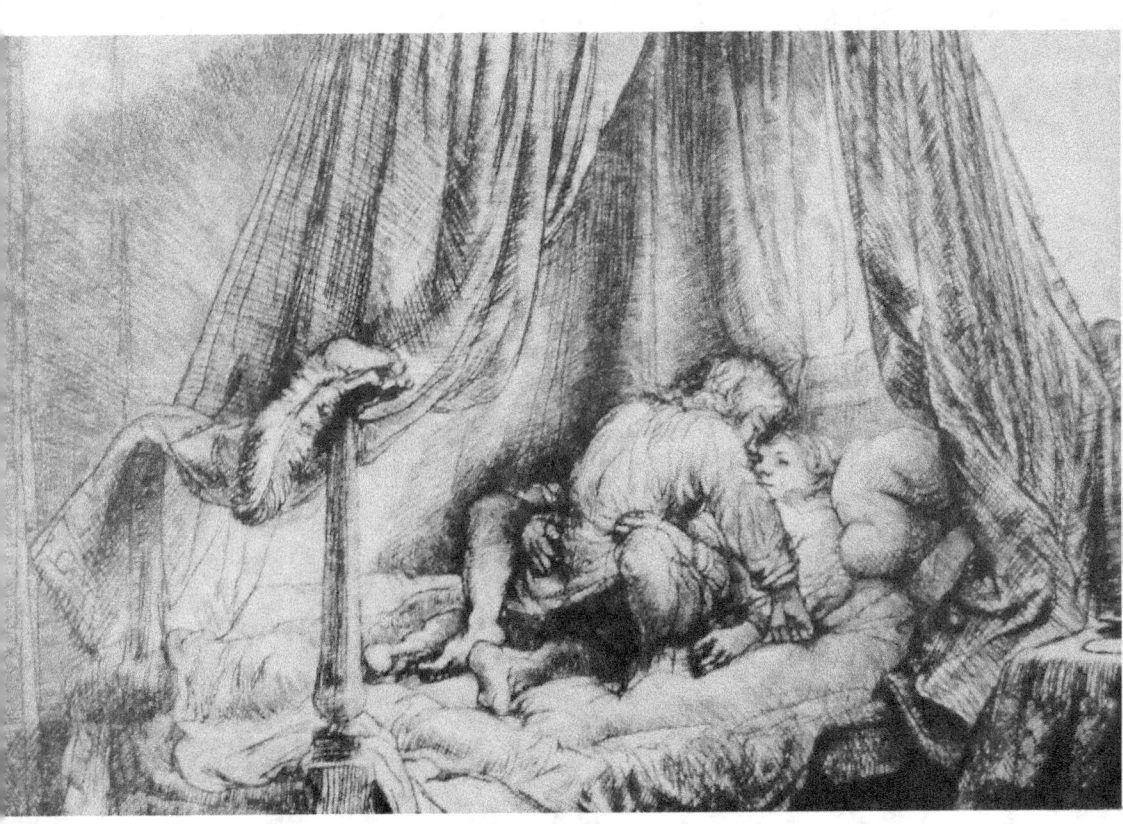

Rembrandt van Rijn, Ledakant, 1646

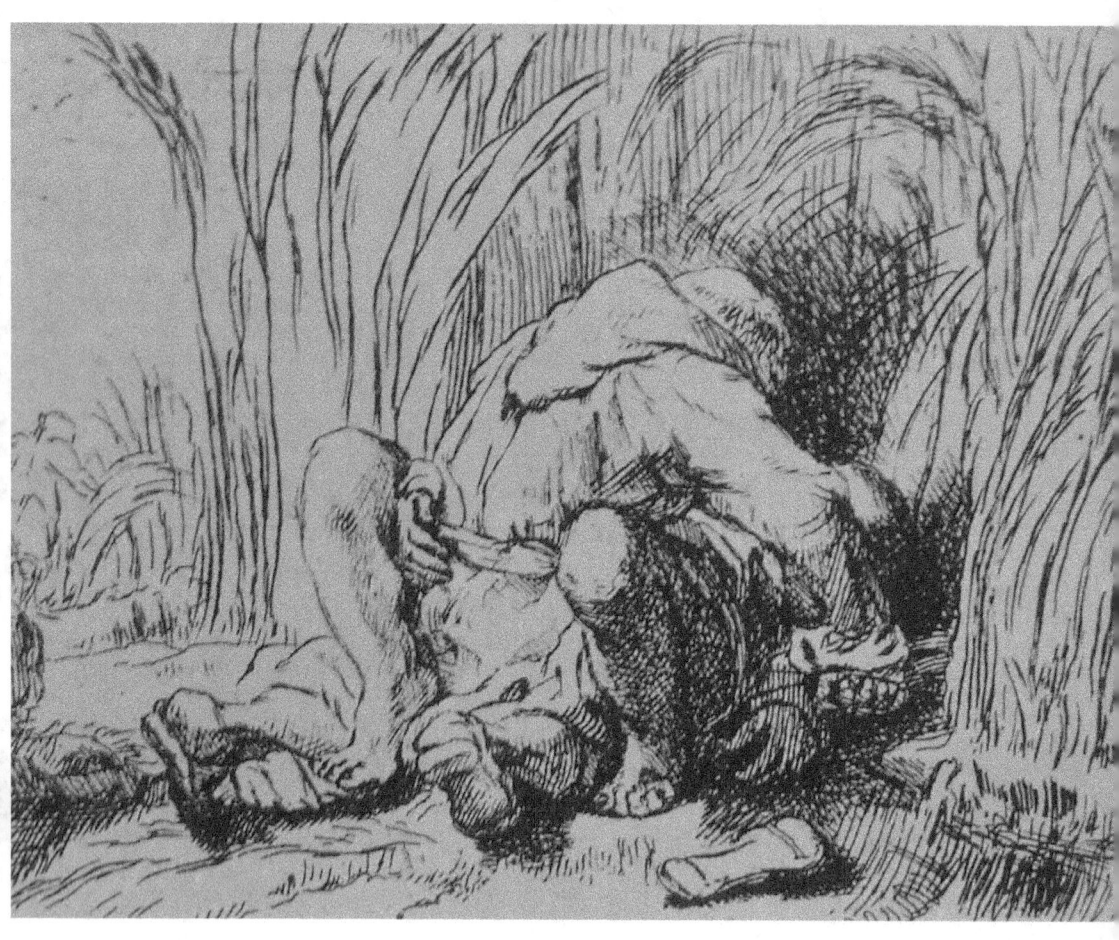

Rembrandt van Rijn, The Monk In the Cornfield

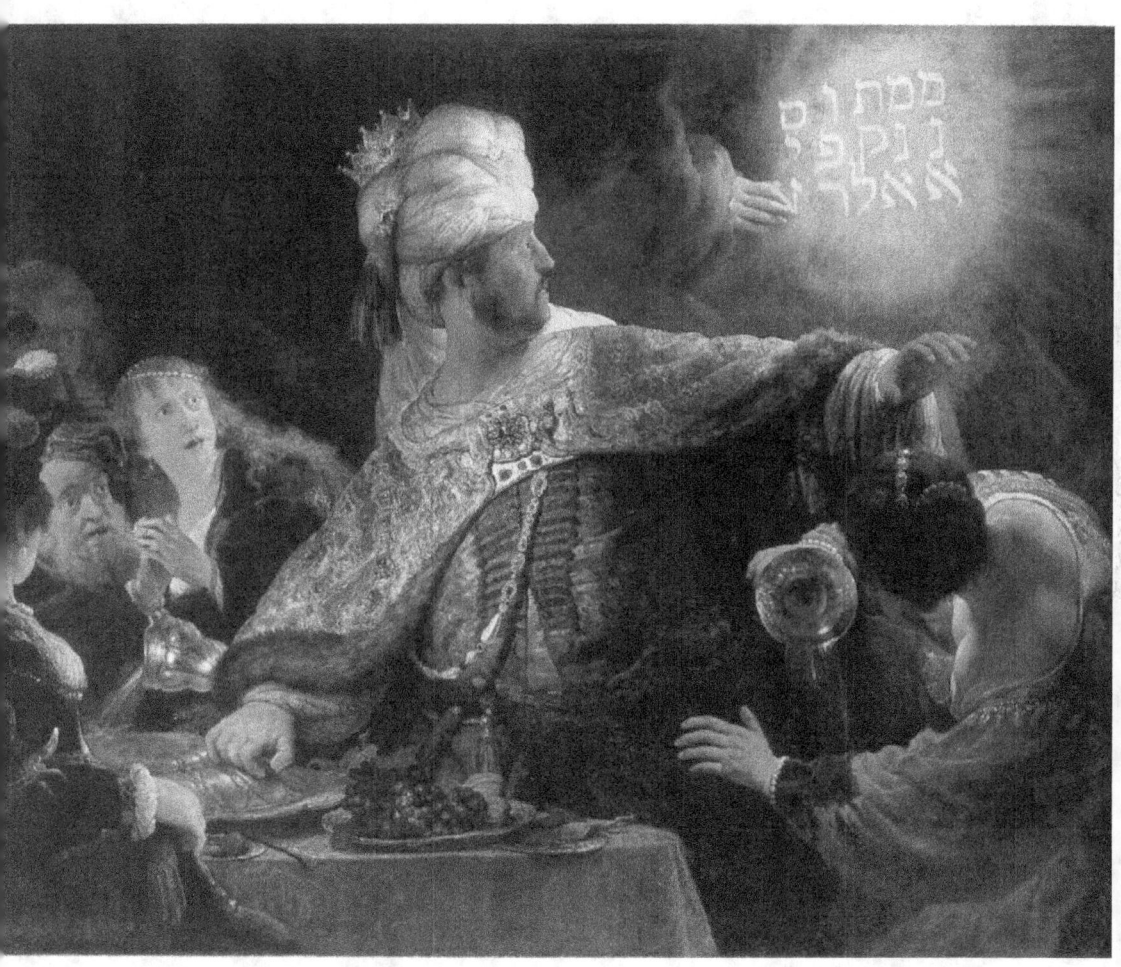

Rembrandt van Rijn, Belshazzar's Feast, 1635, National Gallery, London

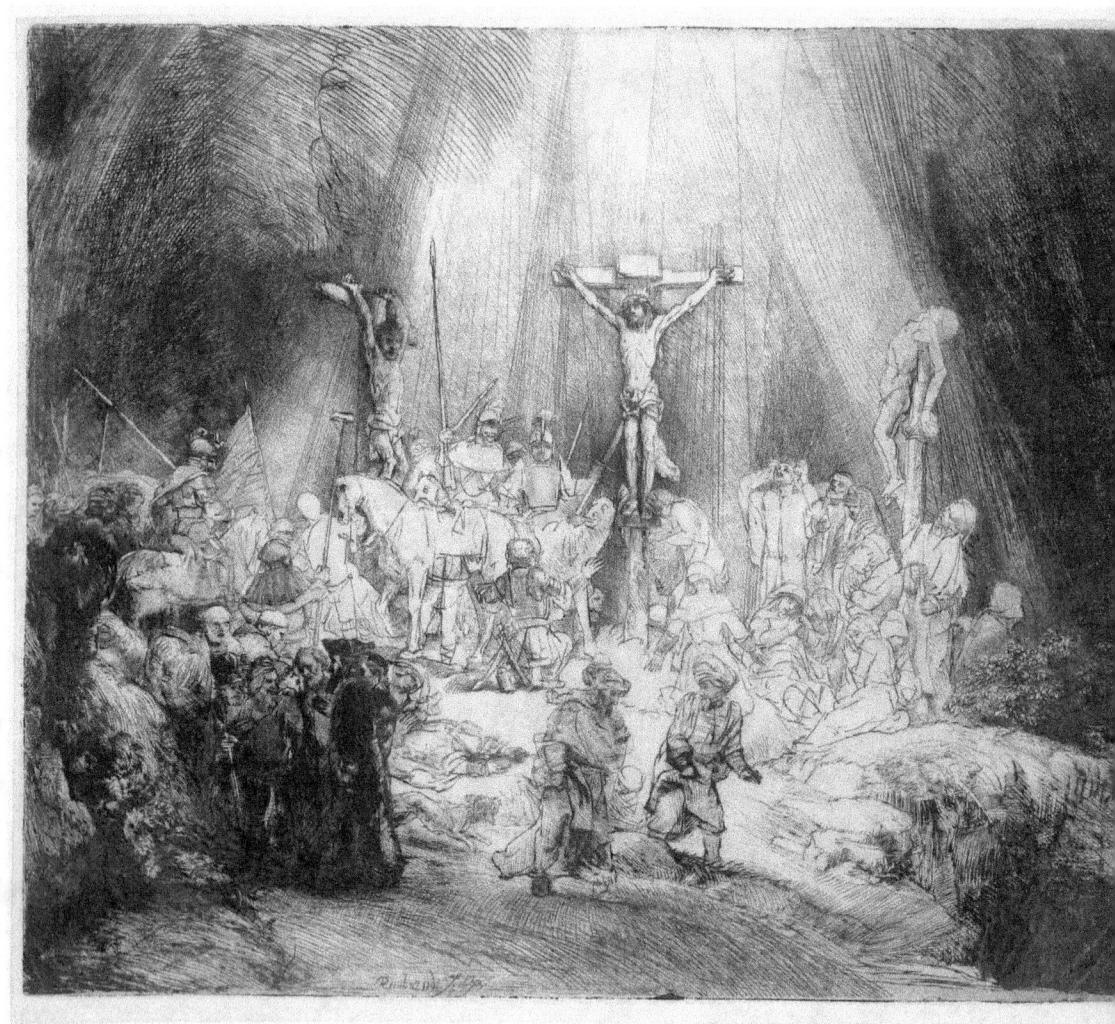

Rembrandt, The Three Crosses, 1653

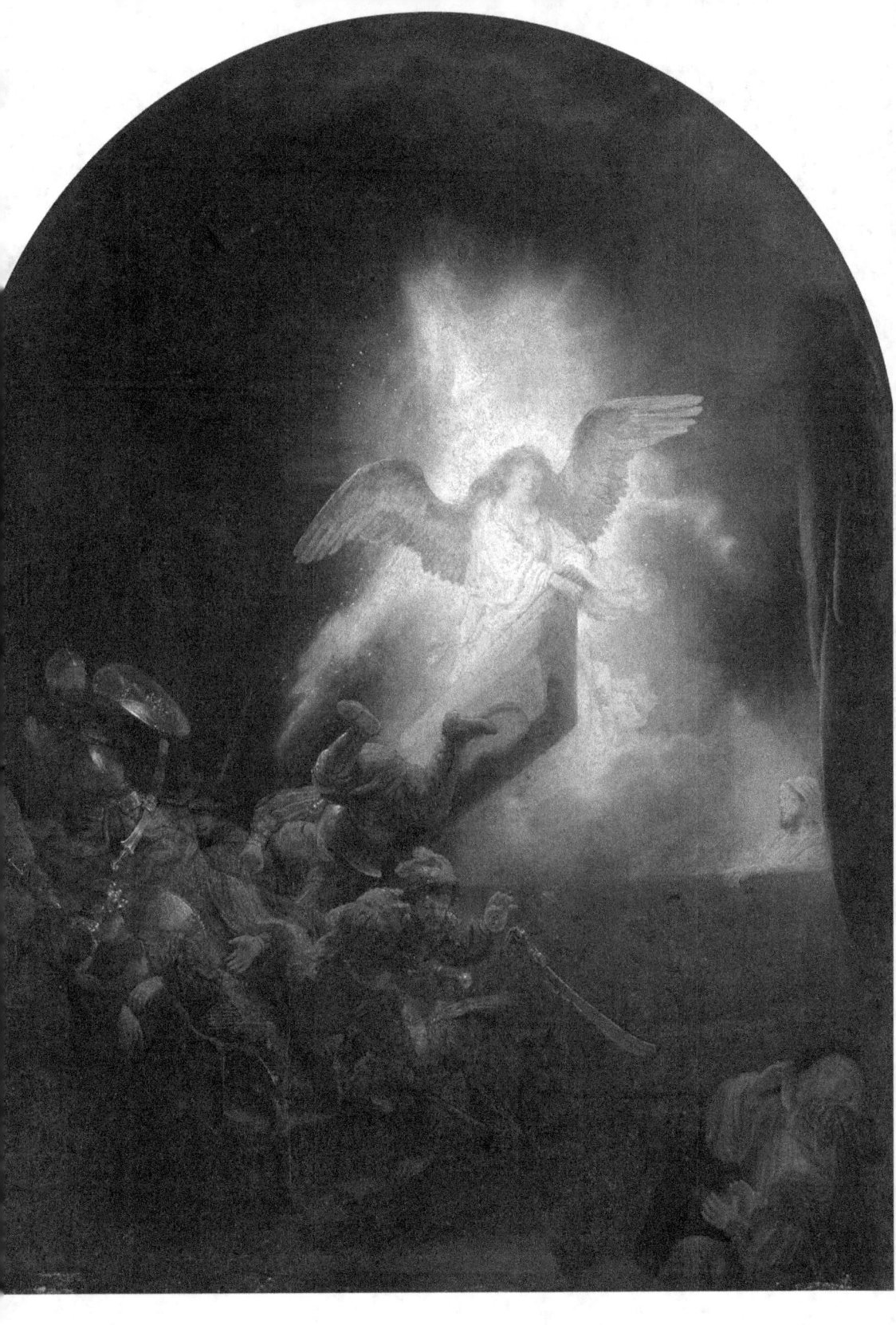

Rembrandt, The Resurrection

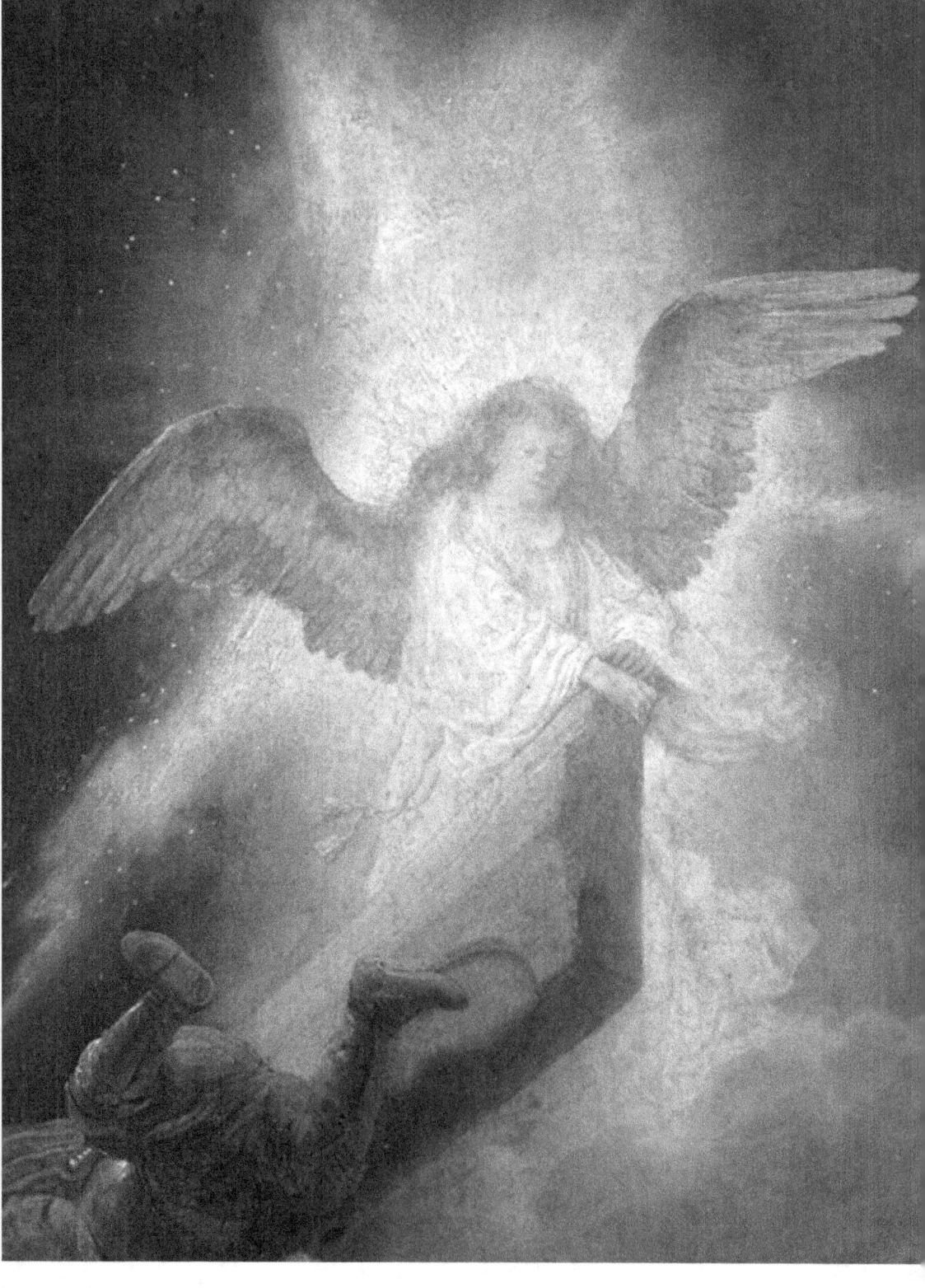

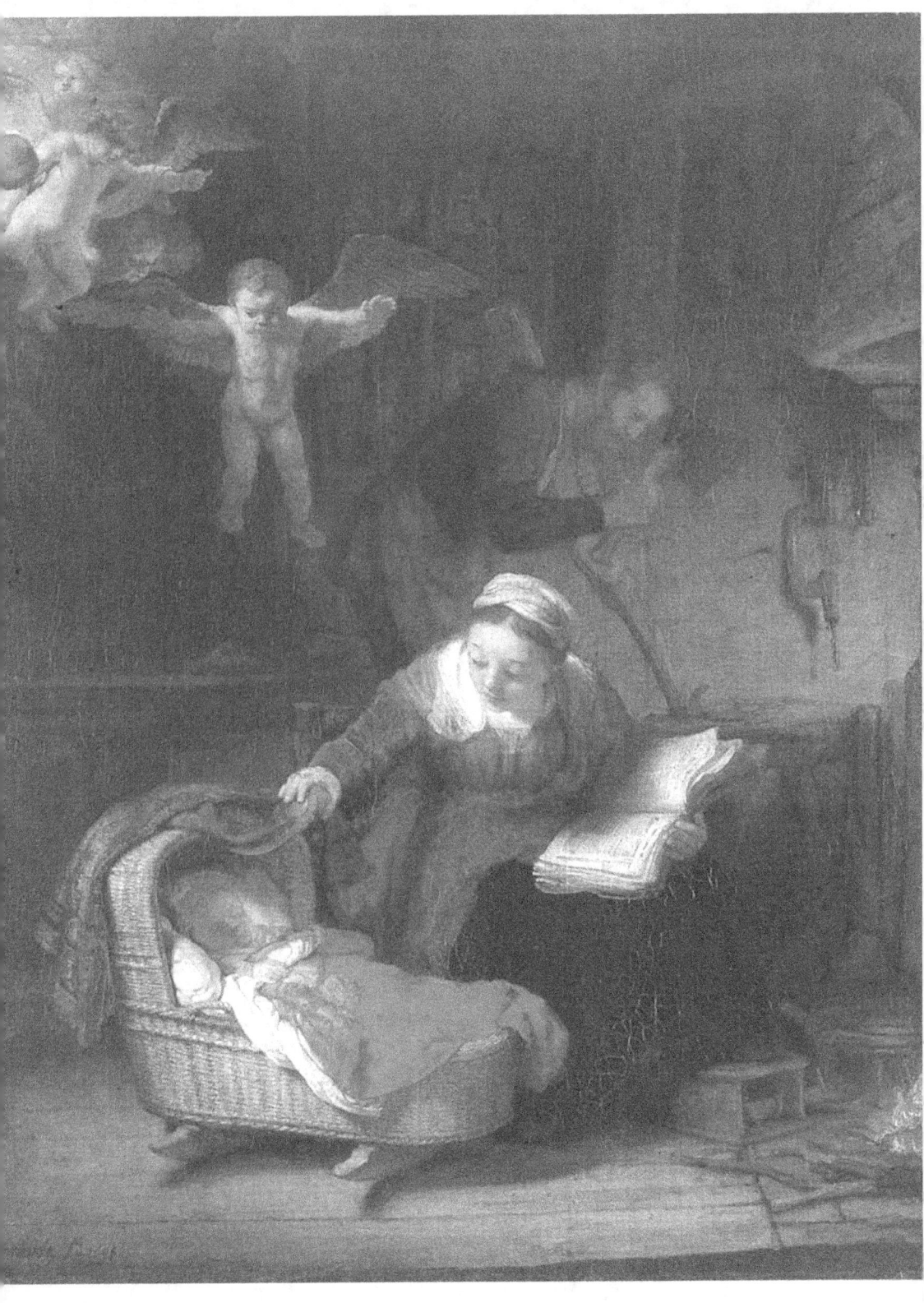

Rembrandt van Rijn, The Holy Family With Angels, 1645, Hermitage Museum

COMPLETE CHRONOLOGICAL LIST OF THE ETCHINGS OF REMBRANDT

Here re-printed from Hind's *Rembrandt's Etchings* (London, 1912) by special arrangement with the publishers, Methuen & Co.1

ABBREVIATIONS, ETC.

h. – head

b. – bust

r. – right

l. – left

S. – signed

D. – dated

ab. – about

R. – Rembrandt

Imp. – impression

I S., V S., etc. – first state, fifth state, etc.

2 S., 7 S., etc. – two states, seven states, etc.

When no number of states is given there is but one.

Mod. – Modern impression. (This does not count as a state.)

† – of doubtful authenticity. [only.]

The sizes are of the plates, – not of the etched surface.

When the states vary in size that of the first state alone is given.

The sizes are given in millimeters. 25 millimeters equal about 1 inch.

1 R's Mother: h. & b. three-quarters r. (After I S. S. & D.), 1628. 2 S. 66 x 63

2 R's Mother: h. only, full face. (After I S. S. & D.). 1628. 2 S. 85 x 72

2* R. With a Broad Nose. Ab. 1628. 70 x 58

3 R. Bareheaded, with high curly hair: h. & b. Ab. 1628. 90 x 72

4 R. Bareheaded: large plate roughly etched: h. & b. S. & D. (in reverse) 1629. 178 x 154

4* Aged Man of Letters. Ab. 1629. 238 x 200

5 Peter and John at Gate of Temple: roughly etched. Ab. 1629-30, 221 x 170

6 Small Lion Hunt (with one lion). Ab. 1629-30. 158 x 118

7 Beggar Man and Beggar Woman Conversing. S. & D., 1630. 2 S. Mod. 78 x 66

8 Beggar Seated Warming Hands at Chafing Dish. Ab. 1630. 2 S. 78 x 46

9 Beggar Leaning on Stick, facing l. Ab. 1630. 85 x 46

10 Beggar in Long Cloak, sitting in arm-chair. Ab. 1630.115 x 78

11 Beggar Seated on Bank. S. & D., 1630. 2 S. 116 x 69

12 Beggar with Wooden Leg. Ab. 1630. 3 S. Mod. 114 x 66

13 Beggar Man and Beggar Woman, behind bank. (I, II, III S. S.) Ab. 1630. 7 S. 116 x 84

14 Man in Cloak and Fur Cap, leaning against bank. S. (in reverse). Ab. 1630. Mod. 112 x 78

15 Beggar in High Cap, standing and leaning on stick. Ab.

1630, or later? 2 S. 156 x 120

16 Ragged Peasant with Hands Behind Him, holding stick. Ab. 1630. 5 S. 92 x 77

17 Flight into Egypt: sketch. Ab. 1630. 6 S. 135 x 84

18 Presentation in Temple (with the angel): small plate. S. & D., 1630. 2 S. 120 x 78

19 Circumcision: small plate. Ab. 1630. 88 x 64

20 Christ Disputing with Doctors: small plate. (I & II S. S. & D.), 1630. 3 S. Mod. 109 x 78

21 B. of Man (R's Father?), Full face, wearing close cap. (After I S. S. & D.), 1630. 6S. 97 x 73

22 B. of Man (R's Father?), Wearing high cap, three-quarters r. S. & D., 1630. 3 S. Mod. 105 x 78

23 Bald-Headed Man (R's Father?) Profile r. h. only, b. added afterwards. S. & D. 1630. 3 S. 118 x 97

24 Bald-Headed Man (R's Father?), Profile r.; small b. S. & D., 1630. 2 S, 57 x 43

25 Three Studies of Old Men's Heads. Ab. 1630. 79 x 81

26 B. of Old Man with Flowing Beard and White Sleeve. Ab. 1630. 71 x 64

27 B. of Old Man.with Flowing Beard: h. bowed forward: l. shoulder unshaded. S. & D., 1630. 89 x 75

28 B. of Old Man with Flowing Beard: h. inclined three-quarters r. S. & D., 1630. 98 x 81

29 R. in Fur Cap: dress light, b. S. & D., 1630. 5 S. 92 x 70

30 R. Bareheaded, in sharp light from r.; looking over his shoulder: b. S. & D., 1630. 3 S. 75 x 75

31 R. Bareheaded and Open-Mouthed, as if shouting: b. S. & D. 1630. 3 S. 83 x 72

32 R. in Cap, Open-Mouthed and Staring: b. in outline. S. & D., 1630. 51 x 46

33 R. Bareheaded, with Thick Curling Hair and small white collar: b. S. Ab. 1630. 2 S. 57 x 49

34 R. in Cap, laughing: b. S. & D., 1630. 6 S. 50 x 44

35 R. Bareheaded, leaning forward as if listening: b. Ab.

1630. 67 x 53

36 R. Bareheaded, leaning forward: b. lightly indicated. Ab. 1630-31. 4 S. 61-64 x 48-49

37 H. of Man in Fur Cap, crying out. Ab. 1631. 4 S. 34 x 28

38 Blind Fiddler. S. & D., 1631. 4 S. 78 x 53

39 H. of Man in High Cap: three-quarters r. Ab. 1631. 2 S. 36 x 22

40 Polander Standing with Stick: profile to r. S. & D., 1631. 58 x 21

41 Sheet of Studies of Men's Heads. S. (in reverse). Ab. 1631. 2 S. 98 x 124

41a Old Bearded Man Nearly in Profile to r.: mouth half open. 5 S. (After II S. 36 x 28)

41b Old Man in Fur Coat and High Cap: b. 9 S. (After III S. 36 x 28)

41c Old Man Seen from Behind: Profile to r.: half figure. 6 S. (After II S. 72 x 42)

41d Man in Square Cap, in profile r. 4S. (After II S. 45 x 23)

41e Man Crying Out, three-quarters l.: b. 7S. (After II S. 39 x 34)

42 Diana at the Bath. S. Ab. 1631. 177 x 158

43 Naked Woman Seated on Mound. S. Ab. 1631. 3 S. 177 x 160

44 Jupiter and Antiope: smaller plate. S. Ab. 1631. 3 S. 84 x 112

45 Man Making Water. S. & D. 1631. 2 S. 84 x 49

46 Woman Making Water. S. & D., 1631. 84 x 63

47 B. of Old Bearded Man Looking Down, three quarters r. S. & D., 1631. 2 S. 119 x 117

48 B. of Old Man with Flowing Beard: h. nearly erect: eyes cast down: looking slightly l. S. & D., 1631. 2 S. 67 x 64

49 B. of Old Man with Fur Cap and Flowing Beard: nearly full face: eyes direct. Ab. 1631. 2 S. 62 x 53

50 R's Mother with Hand on Chest: small b. S. & D., 1631. 4S. Mod. 94 x 66

51 R.'s Mother Seated Facing R., in Oriental head-dress: half length, showing hands. S. & D., 1631. 3 S. 145 x 129

52 R.'s Mother Seated at Table Looking R.: three-quarter length. S. Ab. 1631. 4 S. 147 x 130

53 Bearded Man (R.'s Father?) in Furred oriental cap and robe: half length. (After IS. S. & D.), 1631. 4 S. 146 x 130

54 R. Wearing Soft Hat, Cocked: h. only: body added afterwards (On IV-VII S. S. & D.), 1631. 9 S. 146 x 130

55 R. with Long Bushy Hair, h. only. Ab. 1631. 6 S. 90 x 76

56 R. in Heavy Fur Cap: full face: b. S. & D. 1631. 63 x 58

57 R. Wearing Soft Cap: full face: h. only Ab. 1631. 50 x 44

58 R. with Cap Pulled Forward: b, Ab. 1631. 5 S. Mod. 56 x 45

59 R. with Fur Cap, in oval border: b. Ab. 1631 (or earlier). 90 x 53

60† R. with Bushy Hair and Contracted Eyebrows: b. S. & D., 1631. 3 S. 59 x 55

61 R. Bareheaded, light from r.: b. (II S. only. S.) Ab. 1631. 2 S. 65 x 63

62† R. in Slant Fur Cap: b. S. & D., 1631. 2 S. 63 x 56

63 R. in Cloak with Falling Collar: b. S. & D., 1631. 5 S. 64 x 54

64† R. with Jewel in Cap. Ab. 1631. 2 S. 84 x 79

65† B. of Young Man in Cap. (I S. only. S. & D.), 1631. 2 S. 61 x 57

66 R. in Dark Cloak and Cap: b. Ab. 1631. 3 S. 84 x 82

67 R. (?) Scowling, in octagon: h. only. Ab. 1631. 38 x 35

68 Grotesque Profile: man in high cap. Ab. 1631. 4 S. 38 x 25

69 Peasant with Hands Behind Back. S. & D., 1631. 4 S. 59 x 49

70† B. of Snub-Nosed Man in Cap: profile r. S. & D., 1631. 43 x 38

71† B. of Man in Cap, bound round the ears and chin. Ab. 1631. 54 x 38

72 Beggar with Stick, walking, l. S. & D. 1631. 3 S. 82 x 39

73 Beggar with L. Hand Extended. (After I S. S. & D.). 1631. 5

S. 77 x 50

74 Blindness of Tobit: sketch. Ab. 1631. 5 S. 81 x 70

75 Seated Beggar and Dog. (II S. only. S. & D.), 1631. 2 S. 109 x 81

75* Stout Man in Large Cloak. Ab. 1631. 113 x 74

76† Old Woman Seated In Cottage, with string of onions on wall. (II S. only. S. & D.). 1631, 3 S. 128 x 89

77 Leper "Lazarus Klap." (After I S. S. & D, 1631). 6 S. 102 x 76

77* Beggar Man and Beggar Woman. Ab. 1631. 101 x 76

78 Two Beggars Tramping Towards R. (On II S. S.) Ab. 1631. 2 S. 95 x 59

78* Two Studies of Beggars. Ab. 1631. 93 x 74

79 Beggar with Crippled Hand Leaning on Stick R. Ab. 1631. 5 S. 97 x 42

80 Old Beggar Woman with Gourd. Ab. 1631. 2 S. Mod. 102 x 45

81† Beggar Standing Leaning on Stick L.: small plate. (S. Ab. 1631. 42 x 20

82† B. of Old Woman in Furred Cloak and heavy head-dress. S. & D., 1631. 5 S. 58 x 53

83† B. of Old Woman in High Head-Dress bound round chin. Ab. 1631. 2 S. 71 x 72

84† B. of Beardless Man (R.'s Father?) in fur cloak and cap: looking down: three-quarters l. S. & D. (twice), 1631. 3 S. 74 x 58

85† B. of Bald Man (R.'s Father?) in fur cloak looking r. S. & D., 1631. 3 S. 66 x 58

85† B. of Bald Man Looking Down, Grinning. S. & D., 1631. 3 S. 69 x 57

87† B. of Old Bearded Man with High Forehead and close cap. S. & D., 1631. 2 S. 88 x 74

88† B. of Old Man Looking Down, with wavy hair and beard: cap added afterwards. (II S. only. S.) Ab. 1631. 3 S. 57 x 49

89† Small B. of Bearded Man Looking Down, with eyes nearly closed. Ab. 1631? 2 S. 44 x 44

90 Sheet of Studies: h. of R., beggar couple, h.'s of old man and old woman, etc. Ab. 1632. 2 S. 101 x 113

91† R.'s Mother in Widow's Dress and Black Gloves. S. Ab. 1632? Mod. 150 x 114

92 Old Man Seated, with Flowing Beard, fur cap and velvet cloak. S. & D. Ab. 1632. 3 S. Mod. 150 x 129

93 Man Standing in Oriental Costume and plumed fur cap S. & D., 1632. Mod. 107 x 78

94 St. Jerome Praying: arched print. S. & D., 1632. 3 S. 108 x 80

95 Holy Family. S. Ab. 1632. 95 x 71

96 Raising of Lazarus: larger plate. S. Ab. 1632. 12 S. Mod. 366 x 258

97 Rat-Killer. S. & D., 1632. 2 S. 140 x 124

98 Polander Leaning on Stick: profile l. Ab. 1632. 6 S. 82 x 43

99 Turbaned Soldier on Horseback. S. (in reverse). Ab. 1632. 2 S. 81 x 58

100 Cavalry Fight. Ab. 1632-3. 2 S. 108 x 83

101 Good Samaritan. (I V S. only. S. & D.), 1633. 4 S. 258 x 218

102 Descent from Cross: first plate. S. & D., 1633. 516 x 402

103 Descent from Cross: second plate. S. & D., 1633. 5 S. Mod. 530 x 410

104 Joseph's Coat Brought to Jacob. S. Ab. 1633. Mod. 107 x 80

105 Flight into Egypt: small plate. S. & D., 1633. 2 S. 89 x 62

106 Ship of Fortune. S. & D., 1633. 3 S. 111 x 177

107 R.'s Mother in Cloth Head-Dress, looking down: h. only. (After I S. S. & D.), 1633. 3 S. 62 x 58

108 R. in Cap and Scarf: face dark: b. (II S. only. S. & D.), 1633. 2 S. Mod. 146 x ab. 119

109 R. with Raised Sabre: half length. S. & D., 1634. 3 S. 124 x 108

110 R. with Plumed Cap and Lowered Sabre: three-quarter length: afterwards b. in oval. S. & D., 1634. 3 S. Mod. 197 x 162

111 Jan Cornelis Sylvius, Preacher. (?) S. & D. 1634. 2 S. Mod. 167 x 140

112 R.'s Wife Saskia, with pearls in her hair, b. S. & D., 1634. 86 x 66

113 Woman Reading. S. & D., 1634. 3 S. 123 x 100

114 Peasant, One of Pair, Calling Out. S. & D., 1634. 112 x 43

115 Peasant: Other of Pair, Replying. S. & D., 1634). 111 x 93

116 Two Tramps, Man and woman. Ab. 1634. 62 x 47

117 Sheet of Two Slight Studies: one of two peasants Ab. 1634. 45 x 75

118 Joseph and Potiphar's Wife. S. & D., 1634. 2S. Mod. 90 x 114

119 St. Jerome Reading. S. & D., 1634. 2 S. 108 x 89

120 Angel Appearing to Shepherds. (After I S. S. & D.), 1634. 3 S. Mod. 262 x 21

121 Christ at Emmaus: smaller plate. S. & D., 1634. 101 x 71

122 Christ and Woman of Samaria: among ruins. S. & D., 1634. 2 S. Mod. 121 x 106

123 Crucifixion; small plate. S. Ab. 1634. Mod. 95 x 67

124 Tribute-Money. Ab. 1634. 2 S. Mod. 73 x 103

125 Stoning of St. Stephen. S. & D., 1635. Mod. 95 x 85

126 Christ Driving Money-changers from Temple. S. & D., 1635. 2 S. Mod. 135 x 167

127 Girl with Hair Falling on Shoulders (The "Great Jewish Bride.") (After I. S. S. & D., in reverse). 1635. 4 S. 220 x 168

128 Jan Uytenbogaert, Preacher of sect of Arminian Remonstrants. (After II S. S. & D.), 1635. 6 S. Mod. 250 x 187

129 Old Woman Sleeping. Ab. 1635-7. 69 x 52

130 Old Bearded Man in High Fur Cap, with closed eyes. S. (also S. with initial R. in reverse). Ab. 1635. Mod. 112 x 100

131 First Oriental H. (R.'s father?) S. & D., 1635. 2 S. Mod. 150 x 124

132 Second Oriental H. (R.'s father?) S. Ab. 1635. 150 x 125

133 Third Oriental H. S. & D., 1635. 155 x 134

134 Fourth Oriental H. S. (with initial R.) Ab. 1635. 3 S. 158 x 135

135† H. of Old Man in High Fur Cap. Ab. 1635. 44 x 32

136 Bald Old Man with Short Beard, in profile r. Ab. 1635. 2 S. 66 x 56

137† Curly-Headed Man with Wry Mouth. Ab. 1635. 2 S. 64 x 60

138 Polander Standing with Arms Folded. Ab. 1635. 2 S. 51 x 47

139 Quacksalver. S. & D., 1635. 77 x 36

140 St. Jerome Kneeling in Prayer, Looking down. S. & D., 1635. Mod. 114 x 80

141 Pancake Woman. S. & D., 1635. 6 S. Mod. 109 x 79

142† Strolling Musicians. Ab. 1635. 2 S. Mod. 139 x 116

143 Christ Before Pilate: large plate. S. & D., 1635-6. 5 S. 550 x 446

144 R. and His Wife Saskia: busts. S. & D., 1636. 2 S. Mod. 104 x 95

145 Studies of H. of Saskia and Others. S. & D., 1636. Mod. 151 x 127

146 Samuel Manasseh Ben Israel, Jewish author. S. & D., 1636. 3 S. 149 x 107

147 Return of the Prodigal Son. S. & D., 1636. Mod. 156 x 136

148 Abraham Caressing Isaac. S. Ab. 1637. 2 S. Mod. 116 x 89

149 Abraham Casting Out Hagar and Ishmael. S. & D., 1637. 125 x 95

150 Bearded Man Wearing Velvet Cap with Jewel Clasp. S. & D., 1637. 95 x 83

151 Young Man in Velvet Cap with books beside him. S. & D., 1637. 2 S. 96 x 83

152 Three Heads of Women, one asleep. S. & D. 1637. 2 S. Mod. 142 x 97

153 Three Heads of Women, one lightly etched. Ab. 1637. 2 S. 127 x 102

154 Study of Saskia as St. Catherine (The "Little Jewish Bride.") S. & D. (in reverse), 1638. 110 x 78

155 Sheet with Two Studies: A tree and upper part of h. wearing velvet cap. H. Ab. 1638: tree possibly later. 78 x 67

156 R. in Velvet Cap and Plume, with an embroidered dress: b. S. & D., 1638. Mod. 134 x 103

157 R. in Flat Cap, with shawl about shoulders. Ab. 1638. 2 S. Mod. 93 x 62

158 Man in Broad-Brimmed Hat and Ruff. S. & D., 1630 (or 1638). Mod. 78 x 64

159 Adam and Eve. S. & D., 1638. 2 S. 161 x 116

160 Joseph Telling His Dreams. S. & D., 1638. 3 S. Mod. 110 x 83

161 Death of Virgin. S. & D., 1639. 4 S. Mod. 409 x 315

162 Presentation in Temple: oblong print. Ab. 1639, 3 S. Mod. 213 x 290

163 Sheet of Studies, with woman lying ill in bed. etc. Ab. 1639. 135 x 151

164 Peasant in High Cap, standing leaning on stick. S. & D., 1639. Mod. 83 x 44

165 Death Appearing to a Wedded Couple from Open Grave. S. & D., 1639. 109 x 78

166 Skater. Ab. 1639. 61 x 58

167 Jan Uytenbogaert, Receiver-general (The "Gold-Weigher"). S. & D., 1639. 3 S. Mod. 250 x 204

168 R. Leaning on Stone-Sill: half-length. S. & D., 1630. 3(?) S. 205 x 164

169 Old Man Shading Eyes with Hand. Ab. 1639. 2 S. 134 x 114

170 Old Man with Divided Fur Cap. S. & D., 1640. 3 S. 149 x 137

171 Beheading of John the Baptist. S. & D., 1640 2S. Mod. 128 x 103

172 Triumph of Mordecai. Ab. 1640, or later. 174 x 215

173 Christ Crucified Between Two Thieves: oval plate. Ab. 1640, or later. 2 S. Mod. 135 x 100

174 Sleeping Puppy. Ab. 1640? 3 S. 64 x 105

175 Small Gray Landscape: House and trees beside pool. Ab. 1640. 38 x 82

176 View of Amsterdam. Ab. 1640 (or earlier) 2 S. 112 x 153

177 Landscape with Cottage and Hay Barn: oblong. S. & D., 1641. 129 x 321

178 Landscape with Cottage and Large Tree. S. & D., 1641 125 x 320

179 Windmill. S. & D., 1641. 144 x 207

180 Small Lion Hunt, with two lions. Ab. 1641. 2S. 154 x 121

181 Large Lion Hunt. S. & D., 1641. 2 S. 224 x 300

132 Baptism of Eunuch. S. & D., 1641. 2 S. Mod. 180 x 213

183 Jacob and Laban(?) S. & D. (in reverse), 1641. 2 S. Mod. 144 x 113

184 Spanish Gipsy (Preciosa). Ab. 1641. 133 x 113

185 Angel Departing from Family of Tobias. S. & D., 1641. 3 S. Mod. 103 x 154

186 Virgin and Child in Clouds. S. & D., 1641. 166 x 104

187 Cornelis Claesz Anslo, Mennonite preacher. S. & D., 1641. 5 S. 186 x 157

188 Portrait of Boy, in profile. S. & D., 1641. 93 x 66

189 Man at Desk, wearing cross and chain. S. & D., 1641. 4 S. 154 x 102

190 Card Player. S. & D. 1641. 3 S. Mod. 90 x 81

191 Man Drawing from Cast. Ab. 1641. 2 S. Mod. 93 x 64

192 Woman at Door-Hatch Talking to Man and Children (The "Schoolmaster.") S. & D., 1641. Mod. 94 x 63

193 Virgin with Instruments of Passion. Ab. 1641. 2 S. 110 x 88

194 Man in Arbour. S. & D., 1642. 72 x 56

195 Girl with Basket. Ab. 1642. 2 S. 86 x 63-60

196 Sick Woman with Large White Head-Dress (Saskia). Ab. 1642. 61 x 51

197 Woman in Spectacles, Reading. Ab. 1642. 77 x 67

198 Raising of Lazarus; smaller plate. S. & D, 1642. 2 S. Mod. 150 x 115

199 The Descent from Cross: sketch. S. & D., 1642. 148 x 115

200 Flute-Player (L'Espiegle). (After I S S. & D.), 1642. 4 S. 177 x 144

201 St. Jerome in Dark Chamber. S. & D., 1642. 2 S. Mod. 150 x 173

202 Student at Table by Candle Light. Ab. 1642. 33. 146 x 132

203 Cottage with White Paling. S. & D., 1642. (Date only in II S.) 2 S. 130 x 158

204 Hog. S. & D., 1643. 2 S. 143 x 154

205 Three Trees. S. & D., 1643. 211 x 280

206 Shepherd and Family. S. & D., 1644. 95 x 67

207 Sleeping Herdsman. Ab. 1644. 78 x 57

208 Rest on Flight: night piece. Ab. 1644. 4S. Mod. 92 x 59

209 Six's Bridge. S. & D., 1645. 3 S. 129 x 223

210 Omval. S. & D., 1645. 2 S. Mod. 185 x 225

211 Boat-House. S. & D., 1645. 4 S. 127 x 133

212 Cottages Beside Canal: with church and sailing boat. Ab. 1645. 2 S. 140 x 207

213 Cottage and Farm Buildings, with man sketching. Ab. 1645. 129 x 208

214 Abraham and Isaac. S. & D., 1645. Mod. 157 x 130

215 Christ Carried to Tomb. S. Ab. 1645. 130 x 107

216 Rest on Flight: lightly etched. S. & D., 1645. 129 x 114

217 St. Peter in Penitence. S. & D., 1645. 181 x 116

218 Old Man in Meditation, leaning on book. Ab. 1645. 132 x 106

219 Beggar Woman Leaning on Stick. S. & D. 1646. 2 S. Mod. 81 x 63

220 Study From Nude: Man seated before curtain. S. & D., 1646. 2 S. 164 x 96

221 Study From Nude: Man seated on ground with one leg extended. S. & D., 1646. Mod. 97 x 166

222 Studies From Nude: one man seated, another standing: with woman and baby lightly etched in background. Ab. 1646. 3 S. Mod. 194 x 228

223 Le Lit a La Francaise (Ledekant). S. & D., 1646. 3 S. 152 x 224

224 Monk in Cornfield. Ab. 1646. 48 x 65

225 Jan Cornelis Sylvius, Preacher: posthumous portrait. S. & D., 1646. 2S. 278 x 188

226 Ephraim Bonus, Jewish Physician. S. & D., 1647. 2S. 240 x 177

227 Jan Asselyn. Painter. S. & D., 16.? 3 S. Mod. 215 x 170

228 Jan Six. (After I S. S. & D.), 1647?. 3 S. Mod. 245 x 191

229 Rembrandt Drawing at Window. (After I S.) S. & D., 1648. 5 S. Mod. 157 x 128

230 Sheet of Studies with H. of R., Beggar man, woman and child. S. 1631 or 1651. 111 x 92

231 Artist Drawing from Model: unfinished plate. Ab. 1648, or later? 2 S. Mod. 231 x 184

232 St. Jerome Beside Pollard Willow. (After I S.) S. & D., 1648. 2 S. 179 x 122

233 Beggars Receiving Alms at Door of House. S. & D., 1648. 2 S. Mod. 164 x 128

234 Jews in Synagogue. S. & D., 1648. 3 S. Mod. 71 x 129

235 Medea: or Marriage of Jason and Creusa. (After III S.) S. & D., 1648. 5 S. 240 x 177

236 Christ, with Sick Around Him, Receiving Little Children ("Hundred Guilder Print.") Ab. 1649. 2 S. Mod. 278 x 389

237 Incredulity of Thomas. S. & D., 1650. 162 x 210

238 Canal with Angler and Two Swans. S. & D., 1650. 2 S. 82 x 107

239 Canal with Large Boat and Bridge. S. & D., 1650. 2 S. 82 x 107

240 Landscape with Cow Drinking. Ab. 1650. 2 S. Mod. 102 x 129

241 Landscape with Hay Barn and Flock of Sheep. S. & D., 1650. 2 S. 83 x 174

242 Landscape with Milk-Man. Ab. 1650. 2 S. 65 x 174

243 Landscape with Obelisk, Ab. 1650. 2 S. 83 x 160

244 Landscape with Trees, farm buildings and tower. Ab. 1650. 4 S. 123 x 318

245 Landscape with Square Tower. S. & D., 1650. 4 S. 88 x 155

246 Landscape with Three Gabled Cottages Beside Road. S. & D., 1650. 3 S. 161 x 202

247 The Bull. S. & D., 165.? 76 x 104

248 The Shell. S. & D., 1650. 2 S. 97 x 132

249 Goldweigher's Field. S. & D., 1651. 120 x 319

250 The Bathers. S. & D., 1651. 2 S. Mod. 109 x 137

251 Clement de Jonghe, Printseller. S. & D., 1651. 6 S. Mod. 206 x 161

252 Blindness of Tobit: larger plate. S. & D., 1651. 161 x 129

253 Flight into Egypt: night piece. S. & D., 1651. 5 S. Mod. 127 x 110

254 Star of the Kings: night piece. Ab. 1652. Mod. 94 x 143

255 Adoration of Shepherds: night piece. Ab. 1652. 8 S. Mod. 149 x 198

256 Christ Preaching ("La Petite Tombe.") Ab. 1652. Mod. 155 x 207

257 Christ Disputing with Doctors: sketch. S. & D., 1652. 3 S. 126 x 213

258 David in Prayer, S. & D., 1652. 3 S. Mod. 143 x 93

259 Peasant Family on Tramp. Ab. 1652. Mod. 112 x 92

260 Faust In Study, Watching Magic Disk ("Dr. Faustus"). Ab. 1652. 3 S. Mod. 209 x 161

261 Titus Van Ryn, R.'s Son. Ab. 1656. 101 x 72

262 Sheet of Studies, with wood and paling. Parts of two heads, horse and cart. Ab. 1652. 108 x 136

263 Clump of Trees with Vista. (After I S.) S. & D., 1652. 2 S. 155 x 210

264 Landscape with Road Beside Canal. Ab. 1652. (74-79) x 209

265 Landscape with Sportsman and Dogs. Ab. 1653. 2 S. 129 x 157

266 The Flight Into Egypt: Altered from "Tobias and the Angel" by Hercules Seghers. Ab. 1653. 7 S. 213 x 284

267 St. Jerome Reading, in Italian landscape. Ab. 1653. 2 S. 260 x 207

268 Jan Antonides Van Der Linden, Professor of Medicine. 1665. 6 S. Mod. (124+49) x 105

269 Lieven Willemsz Van Coppenol, Writing-Master: smaller plate. Ab. 1653. 6 S. 257 x 189

270 Christ Crucified Between Two Thieves: large oblong plate (The "Three Crosses") (After the II S.) S. & D. 1653. 5 S. 385 x 450

271 Christ Presented to People: large oblong plate. (After the V S.) S. & D., 1655. 7 S. 383 x 45

272 Golf-Player. S. & D., 1654. 2 S. Mod. 96 x 144

273 Adoration of Shepherds (with lamp). S. Ab. 1654. 2 S. Mod. 105 x 129

274 Circumcision (in Stable). S. & D., 1654. 3 S. 94 x 144

275 Virgin and Child with Cat: Joseph at window. Mod. S. & D., 1654. 2 S. 94 x 143

276 Flight Into Egypt: Holy Family crossing brook. S. & D., 1654. Mod. 94 x 144

277 Christ Seated Disputing with Doctors. S. & D., 1654. 2 S. 95 x 144

278 Christ Between His Parents, Returning from Temple. S. & D., 1654. 94 x 144

279 Presentation in Temple: Dark manner. Ab. 1654. 210 x 162

280 Descent from Cross: by torchlight. S. & D., 1644. Mod. 210 x 161

281 The Entombment. Ab. 1654. 4S, 211 x 161

282 Christ at Emmaus: larger plate. S. & D., 1654. 3 S. Mod. 209 x 159

283 Abraham's Sacrifice. S. & D., 1655. 156 x 131

284 Four Illustrations to Spanish Book. (On each part after I S.) S. & D., 1655. 5 S. The undivided plate 279 x 160

285 The Goldsmith. S. & D., 1655. 2 S. Mod. 77 x 57

286 Abraham Entertaining the Angels. S. & D., 1656. 159 x 131

287 Jacob Haaring (The "Old Haaring"). Ab. 1655. 2 S. 195 x 149

288 Thomas Jacobsz Haaring (The "Young Haaring"). S. & D., 1655. 5 S. Mod. 197 x 148

289 Arnold Tholinx, Inspector Medical Colleges at Amsterdam. Ab. 1656. 2 S. 198 x 149

290 Jan Lutma, the Elder, Goldsmith and Sculptor. (After I S.) S. & D., 1656. 3 S. Mod. 197 x 148

291 Abraham Francen, Art Dealer. Ab. 1656, or later? 9 S. Mod. 152 x 208

292 St. Francis Beneath Tree, Praying. S. & D., 1657. 2 S. 180 x 244

293 Agony in the Garden. S. & D., 165. (Ab. 1657?) Mod. 118 x 83

294 Christ and Woman of Samaria: arched print. (On III S.) S. & D., 1658. 3 S. Mod. 205 x 160

295 Phoenix; or Statue Overthrown: Allegory of doubtful meaning. S. & D., 1658. 180 x 183

296 Woman Sitting Half Dressed Beside Stove. S. & D., 1658. 7 S. 228 x 186

297 Woman at Bath, with hat beside her. S. & D., 1658. 2 S. 157 x 128

298 Woman Bathing Her Feet at Brook. S. & D., 1658. Mod. 159 x 80

299 Negress Lying Down. S. & D., 1658. 3 S. Mod. 80 x 157

300 Lieven Willemsz Van Coppenol, Writing-Master: larger plate. Ab. 1658. 6 S. Mod. 341 x 290

300* R. Etching. S. & D., 1658. 118 x 64

301 Peter and John Healing Cripple at Gate of Temple. S. & D., 1659. 4S. Mod. 179 x 216

302 Jupiter and Antiope: larger plate. S. & D., 1659. 2 S. 139 x 205

303 Woman with Arrow. S. & D., 1661. 3 S. 203 x 123

LIST OF THE REJECTED ETCHINGS

(In the order of Bartsch and Seidlitz, but with the Hind numbers.)

304 Rembrandt with Falcon. 126 x 98

305 Abraham Casting Out Hagar and Ishmael: coarsely etched. 81 x 57

306 Abraham Casting Out Haagar and Ishmael: delicately etched. 73 x 53

307 Rest on the Flight. 217 x 165

308 Beheading of John the Baptist. S. with R.'s monogram. 158 x 124

309 St. Jerome Kneeling: large plate. 389 x 332

310 Hour of Death. 1644. 138 x 89

311 The Rat-Killer. 124 x 81

312 Woman Cutting Her Mistress's Nails (Bathsheba?). 124 x 95

313 Cupid Resting. 89 x 119

314 Old Man in Turban, Standing with Stick. 138 x 108

315 The Astrologer. S. f. bol. 140 x 117

316 Philosopher in His Chamber. 70 x 51

317 Physician Feeling Pulse of Patient. 70 x 54

318 A Tramp, with Wife and Child. 66 x 70

319 Peasant, Standing. 58 x 35

320 Peasant Woman, Standing. 59 x 36

321 Beggar in Tall Hat and Long Cloak, with cottage and two figures in background. 118 x 86

322 Sick Beggar and Old Beggar Woman. 76 x 56

323 Landscape with Cow; square tower in distance. 72 x 120

324 Village with Two Gabled Cottages on Canal. 56 x 174

325 Landscape with Coach. 64 x 177

326 The Terrace. 163 x 188

327 Clump of Trees Beside Dyke-Road. 75 x 204

323 Orchard with Barn ("Paysage aux deux allées"). 2 S. 91 x 205

329 Village with Ruined Tower. S. & D., J. Koninck. 1663. 100 x 153

330 Landscape with Little Figure of Man.

331 Canal with Cottages and a Boat. 3 S. 166 x 182

332 The Large Tree. 162 x 128

333 Landscape with a White Fence. 90 x 161

334 The Angler in a Boat. 112 x 139

335 Landscape with a Canal and Church Tower. 80 x 180

336 Low House on the Banks of a Canal. Signed P. D. W. 77 x 207

337 The Wooden Bridge. 76 x 207

338 Landscape with Canal and Palisade. D. 1659. 75 x 204

339 The Full Hay-Barn. 99 x 153

340 Cottage with a Square Chimney. 74 x 177

341 House with Three Chimneys.90 x 160

342 The Hay-Wain. 68 x 132

343 The Castle. 79 x 102

344 The Village Street. Signed P. D. W. 81 x 153

345 Unfinished Landscape. Signed P. D. W. 1605 (or 1659). 90 x 162

346 Landscape with Canal, Angler and milk-man. Signed P. D. W. 79 x 206

347 Young Man Seated, with game-bag. D. 1650. 78 x 67

348 Bare-Headed Old Man with Hands upon Book.

349 Bald Old Man in Profile L. 75 x 69

350 Old Man with Beard, in Cap: profile r.: in oval. Mod. 71 x 54

351 Man with Square Beard and Curly Hair. S. with R.'s monogram and D. 1631. 56 x 48

352 Man Crying Out, three-quarters l.: bust.

353 Bust of Man with Thick Lips. 75 x 60

354 Philosopher with Hour-Glass. Wood cut. 55 x 50

355 The Painter. 70 x 63

356 Head of Young Man in Broad-Brimmed Hat: in octagon. 108 x 90

357 Young Man In Broad-Brimmed Hat: lightly etched. 92 x 67

358 Bust of Young Man with Feathers in Hat. 72 x 52

359 Small Head of Man in Ruff, with Feathers in Cap. 31 x 27

360 White Negro. Signed A. de Hae. 120 x 102

361 So-Called Study for Great Jewish Bride. 135 x 97

362 Old Woman Meditating Over Book.

363 Rembrandt's Mother: bust. 79 x 63

364 White Negress. S. with R.'s monogram, in reverse. 112 x 83

365 Head of Old Woman: Cut as far as band round brow. S. with R.'s monogram. 36 x 43

366 Young Woman Reading. 106 x 102

367 Head and Shoulders of Dog: sketched in corner of plate. 118 x 150

368 Slight Study of Woman's Head. 64 x 55

369 Head and Bust of Man with Beard: looking down towards l. 79 x 63

370 View of Amsterdam. 58 x 175

371 Two Cottages with Pointed Gables. 66 x 173

372 Village Divided by Dyke. Signed P. D. W. 76 x 183

373 Angler in Boat. 83 x 182

374 Landscape with Two Anglers. 81 x 180

375 Two Ruined Cottages. 113 x 181

376 Old Barn. 73 x 114

377 Supposed Portrait of Jan Six. 46 x 45

378 Profile of Old Bearded Man in Turban. 45 x 31

379 Profile of Jewish-Looking Old Man in Fur Cap. 47 x 29

380 Old Man with Pointed Beard. 63 x 53

381 Head of Man with Curly Hair and Thin Moustache. 63 x 51

382 Jew Standing. 51 x 40

383 Head of Rembrandt's Mother. 50 x 41

384 Portrait of Rembrandt. 54 x 52

385 Child Asleep. 38 x 40

386 Bathsheba. 146 x 112

387 Old Man in Broad-Brimmed Hat: bust in profile. 51 x 31

388 The Circumcision. (II S. only. S.) Rembrandt fecit. 2 S. 214?(165 – 160)

389 Head of Old M an with Snub Nose: in cap: profile to l. 27 x 21

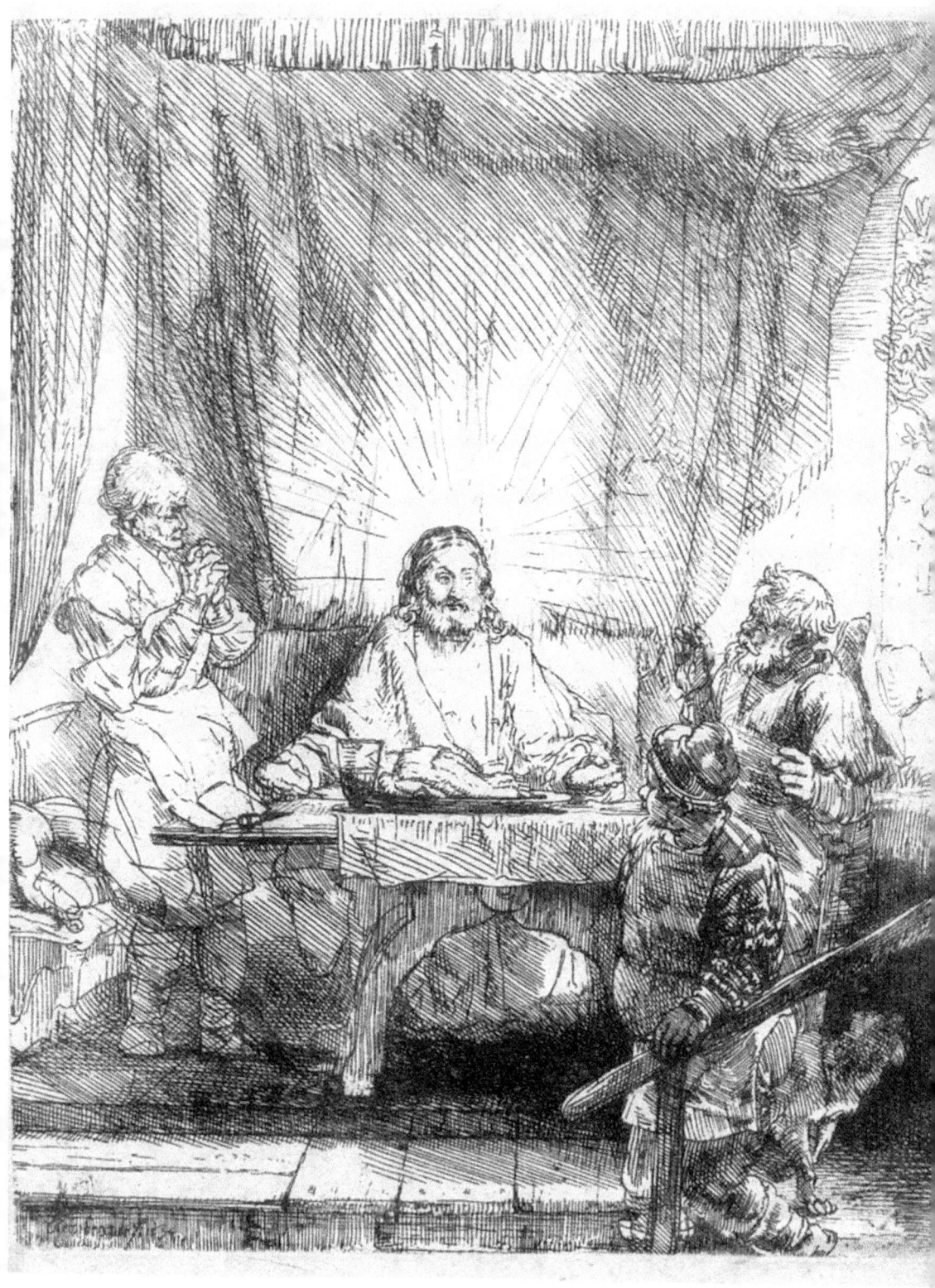

Rembrandt, Christ At Emmaus, 1654

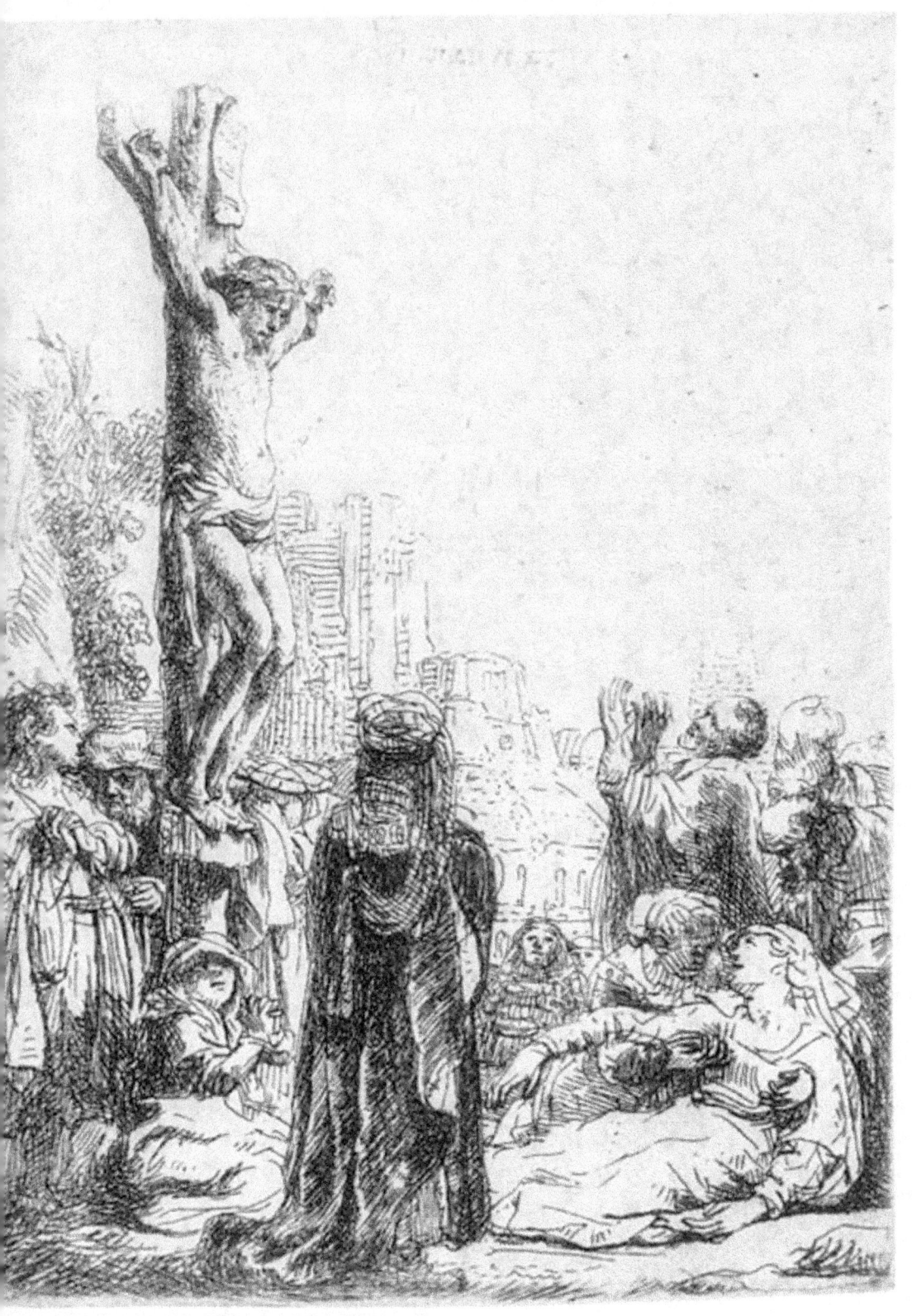

Rembrandt, The Crucifixion, 1637, Vienna

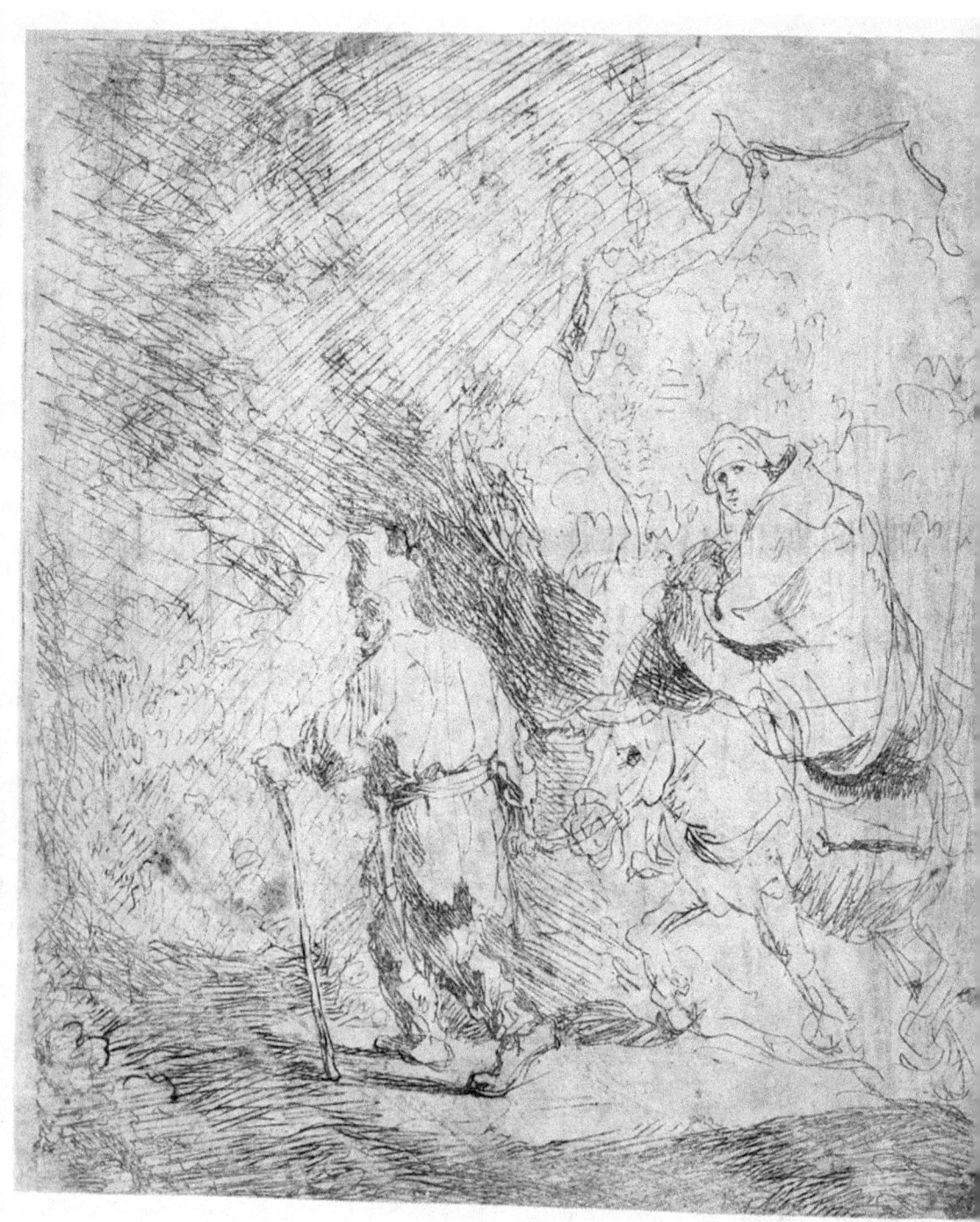

Rembrandt, The Flight Into Egypt, 1627, Rijksmuseum, Amsterdam

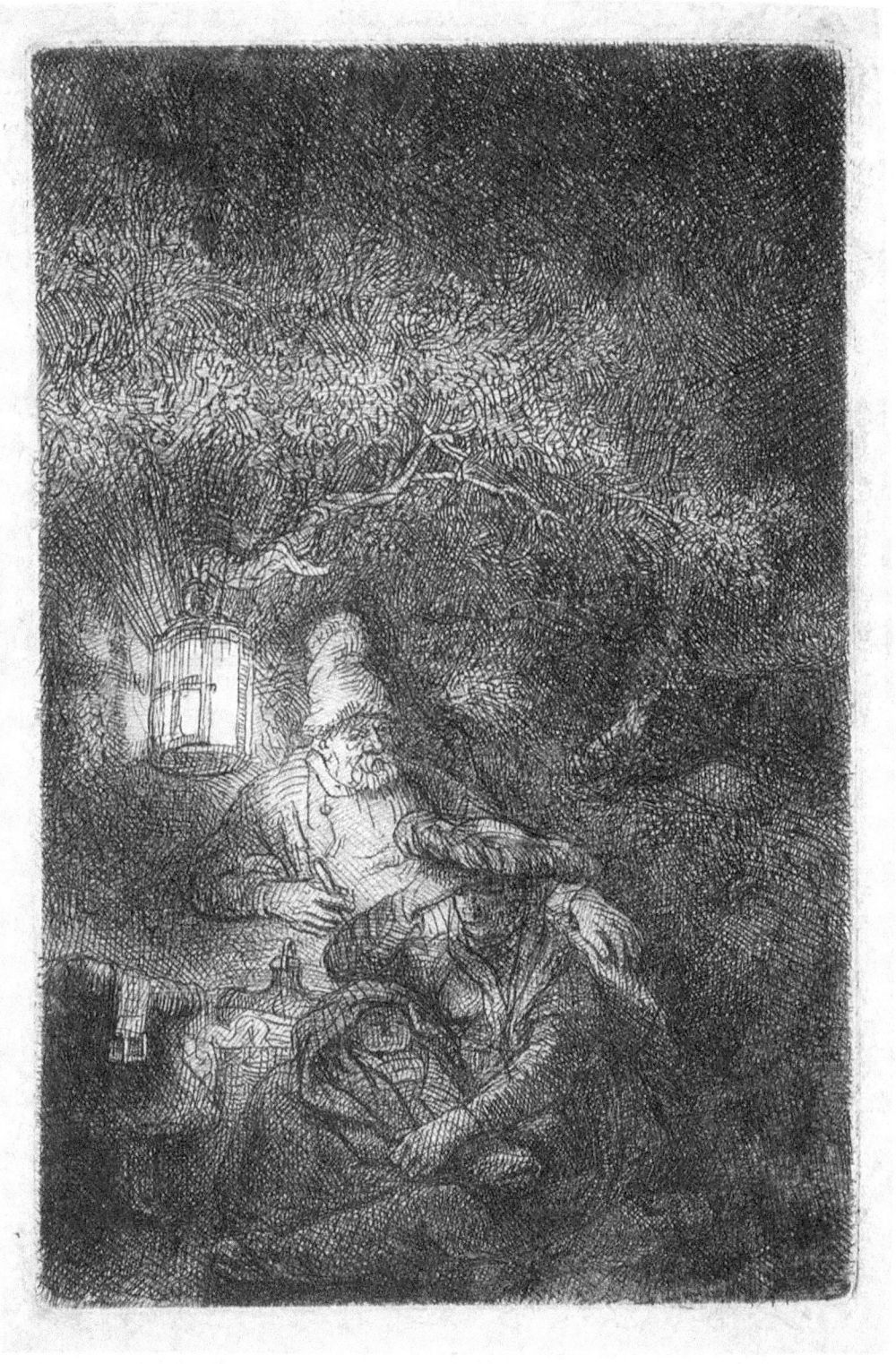

Rembrandt, The Rest on the Flight Into Egypt, Rijksmuseum, Amsterdam

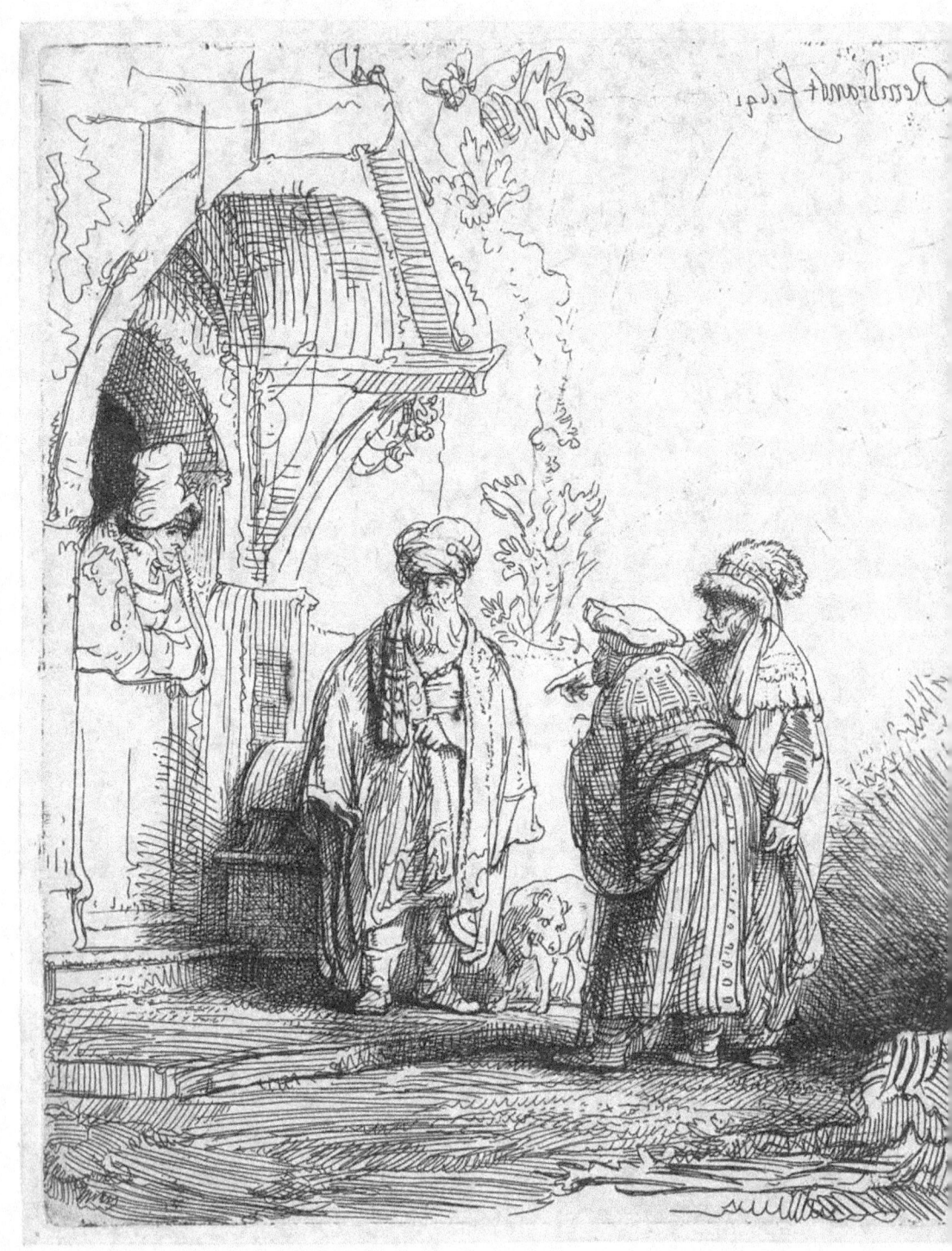

Rembrandt, Jacob and Laban, 1641, Rijksmuseum, Amsterdam

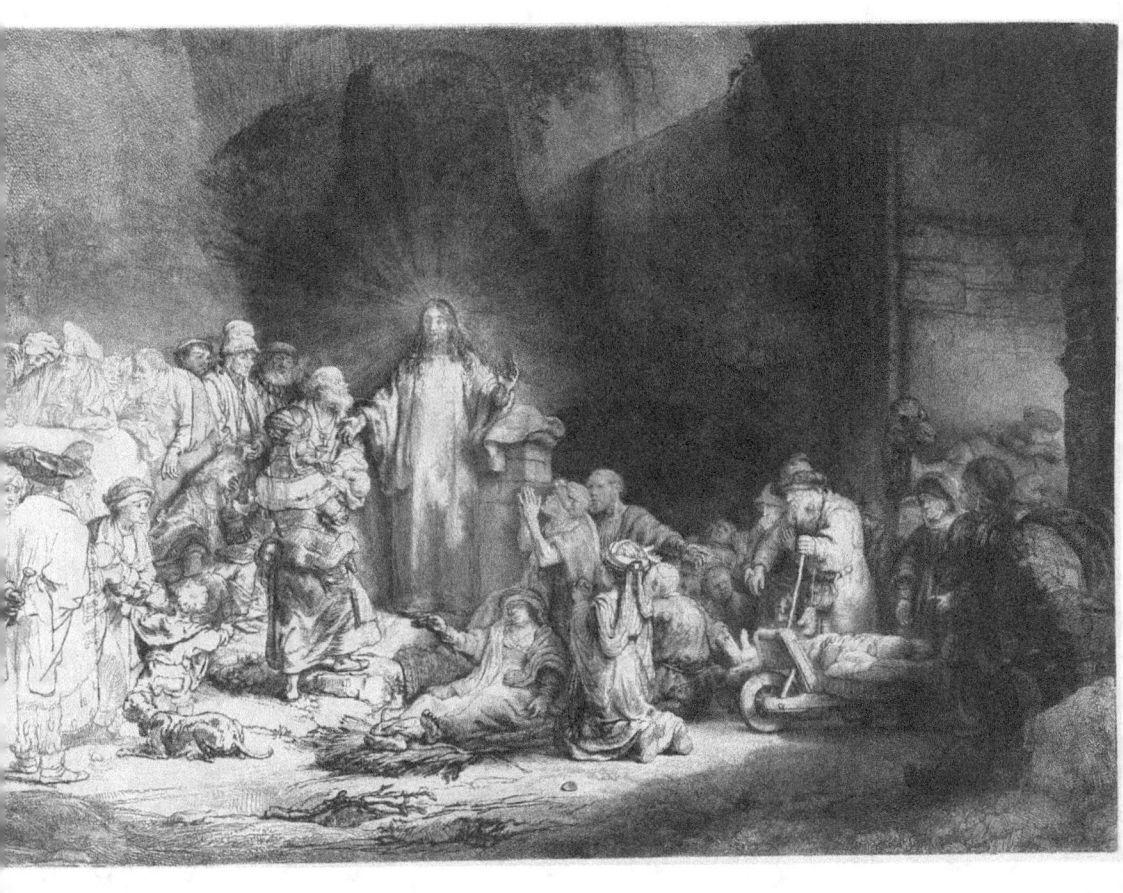

Rembrandt, The Little Children, 1646-50, Rijksmuseum, Amsterdam

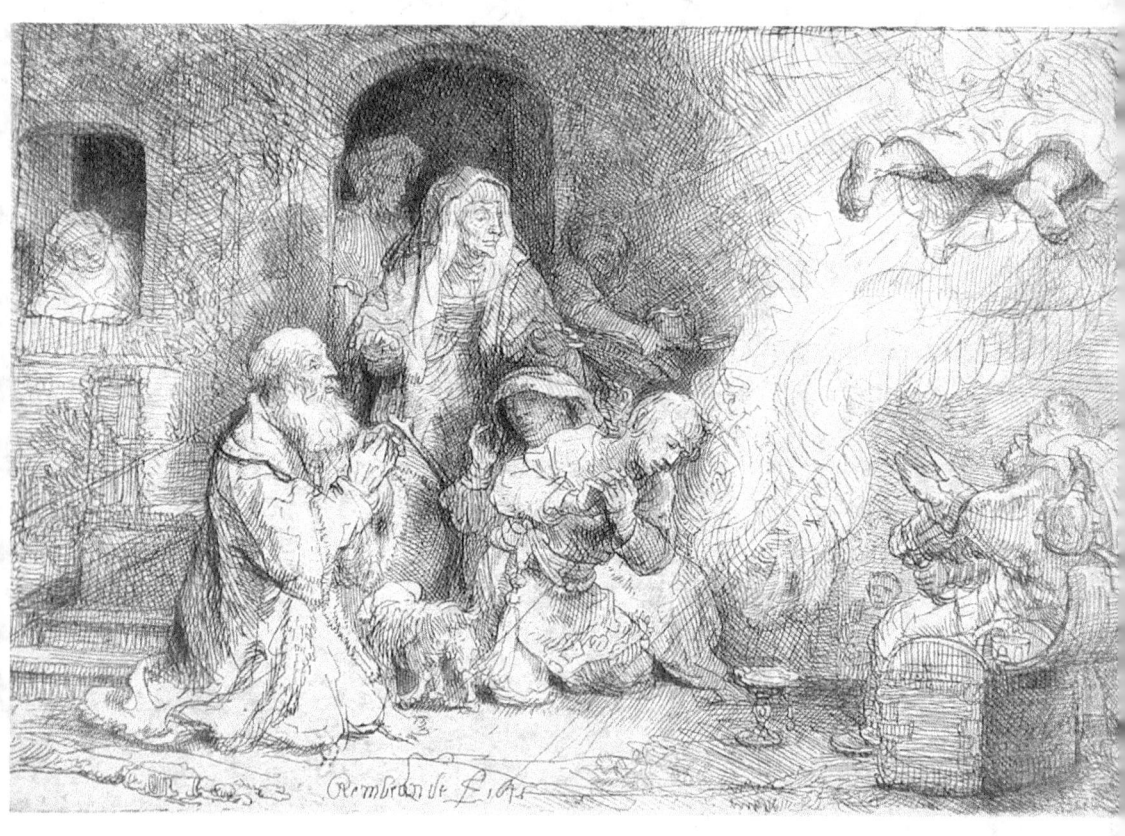

Rembrandt, The Angel Departing From the Family of Tobit, Los Angeles

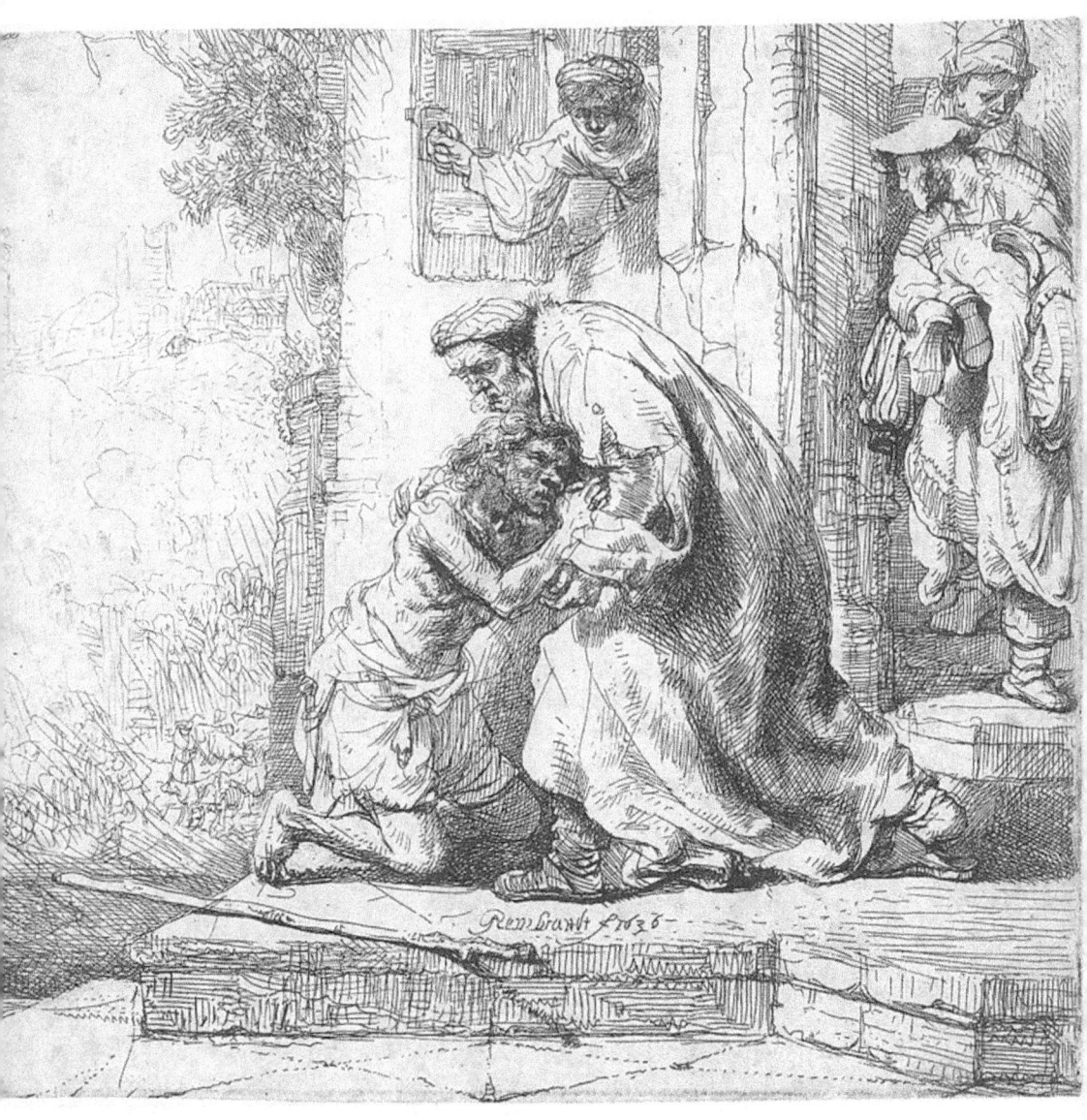

Rembrandt, The Return of the Prodigal Son, 1636, Rijksmuseum, Amsterdam

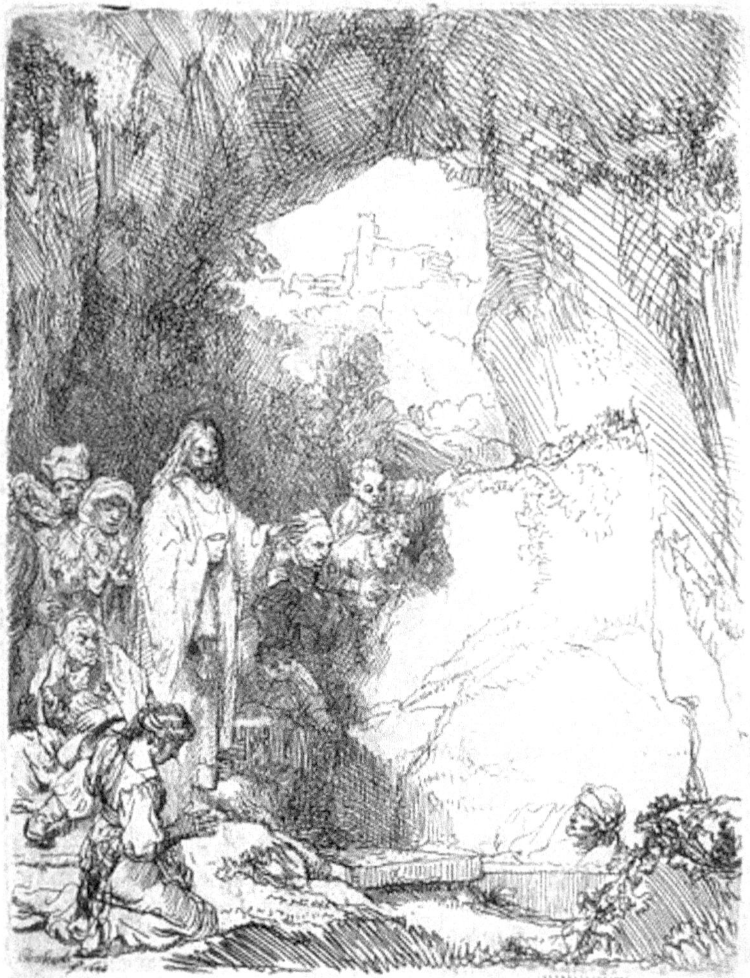

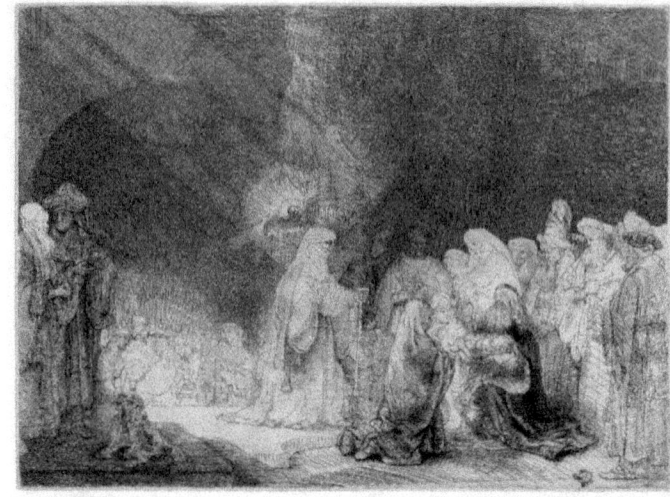

Rembrandt,
The Raising of Lazarus, 1642,
Rijksmuseum,
Amsterdam (above).
The Presentation In the
Temple, 1639,
British Museum (Right).

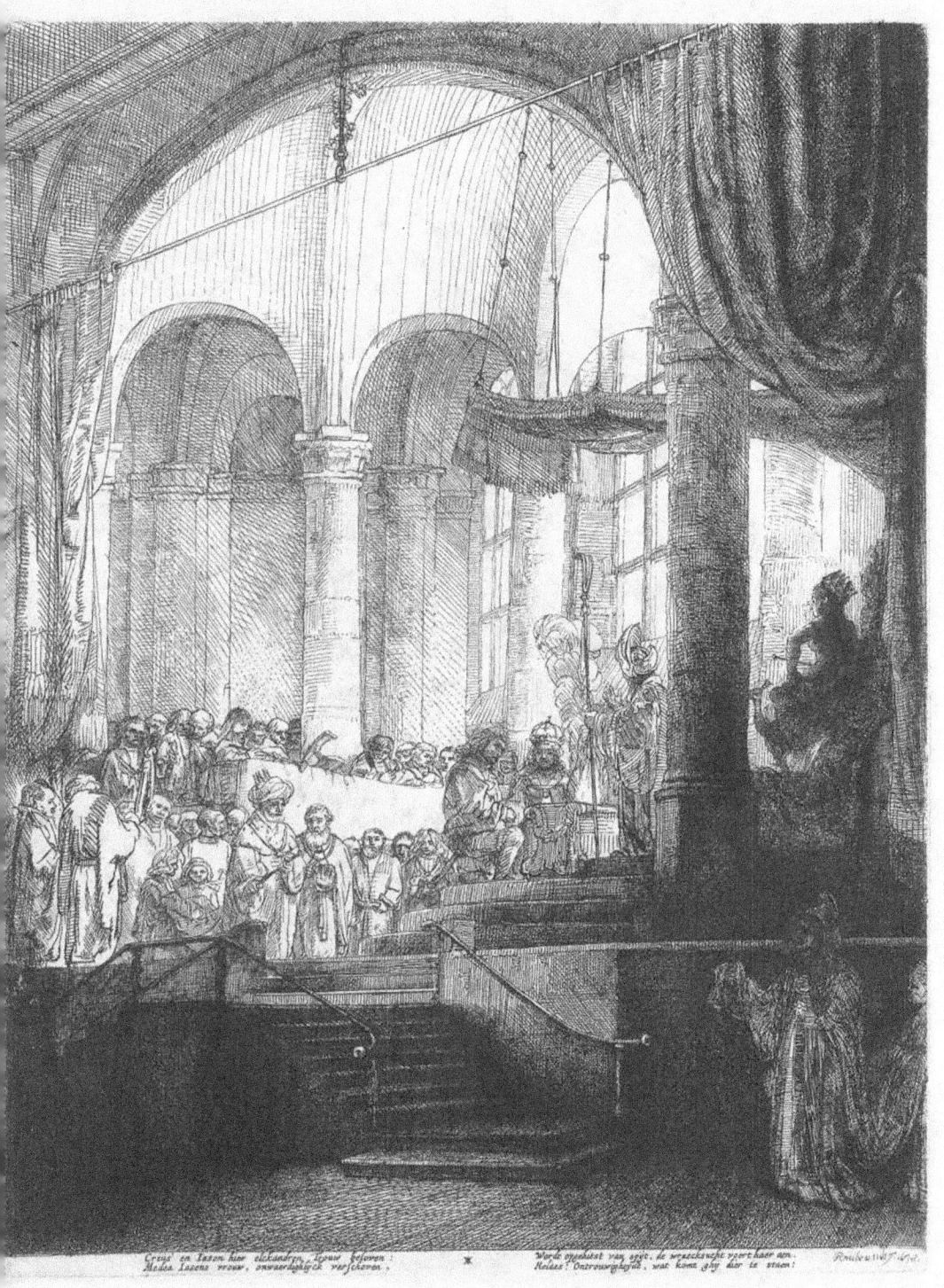

Rembrandt, Medea, 1648, Rijksmuseum, Amsterdam

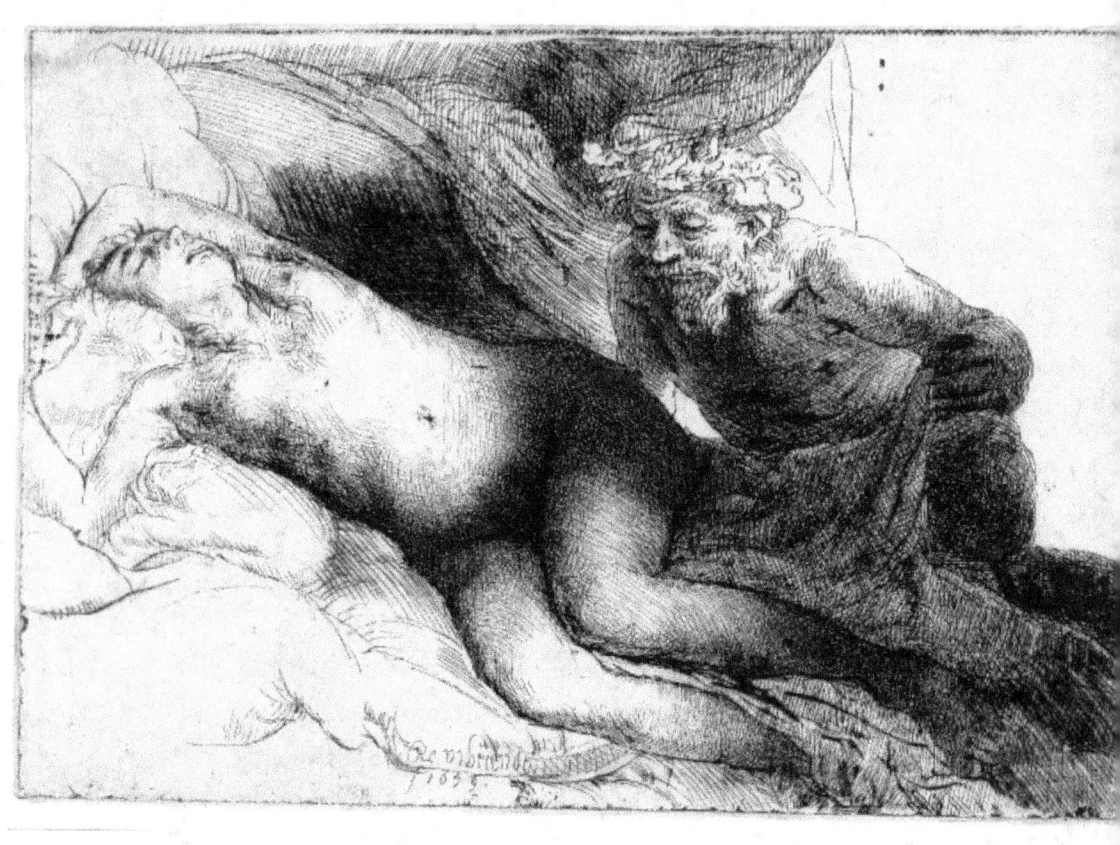

Rembrandt, Jupiter and Antiope, 1659, British Museum

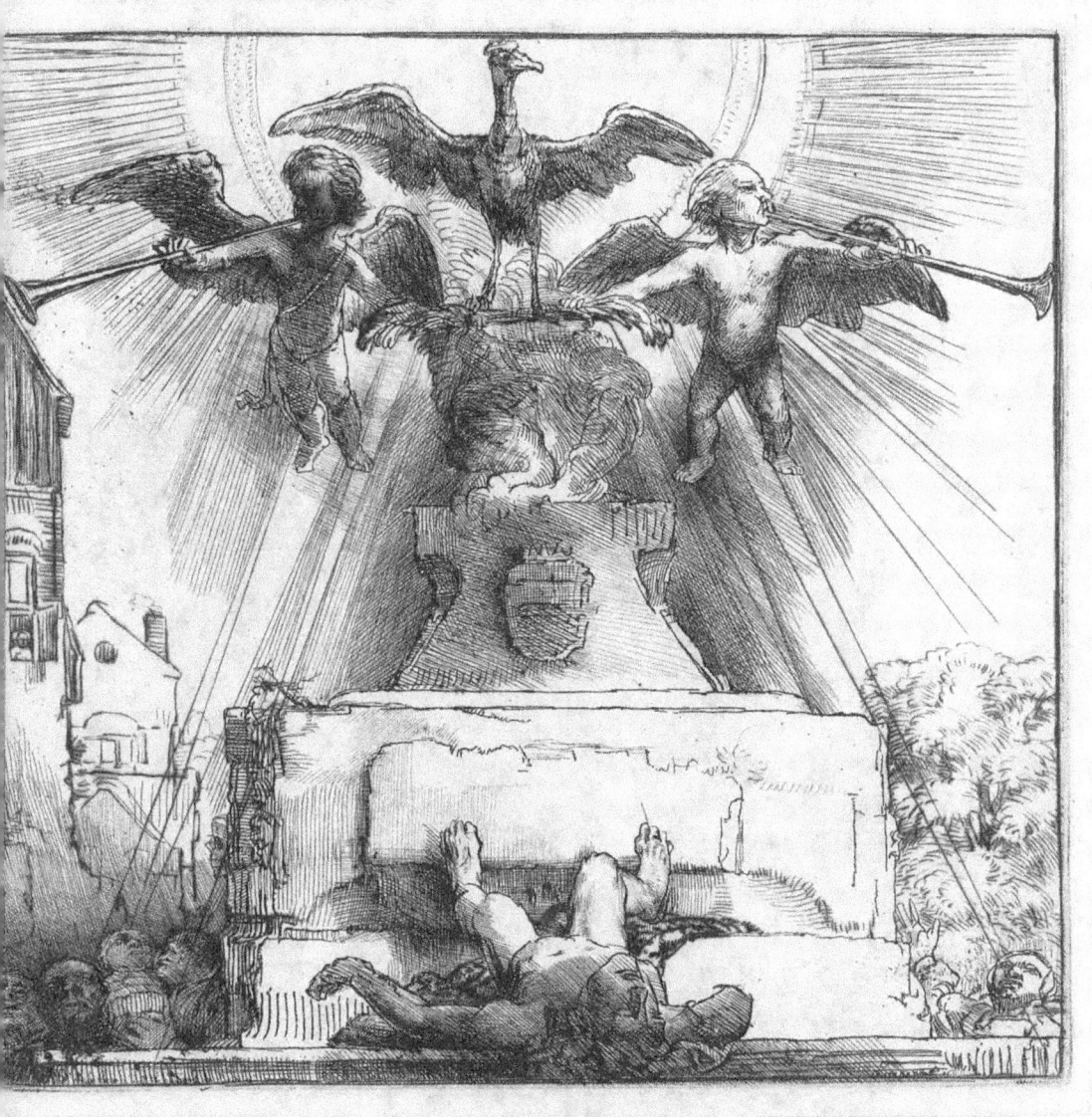

Rembrandt, The Phoenix, or the Statue Overthrown, 1658

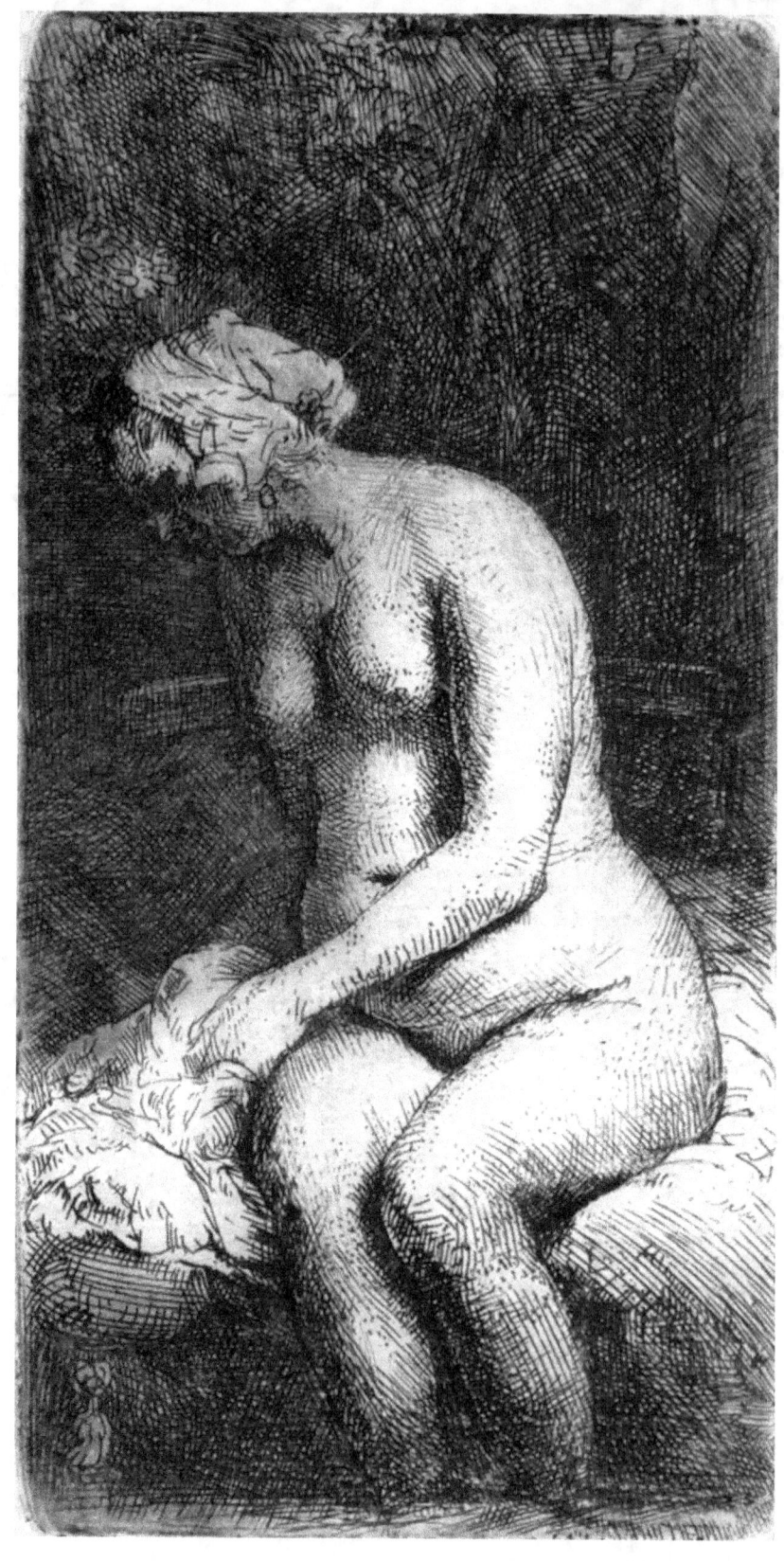

Rembrandt, Seated Nude, 1658

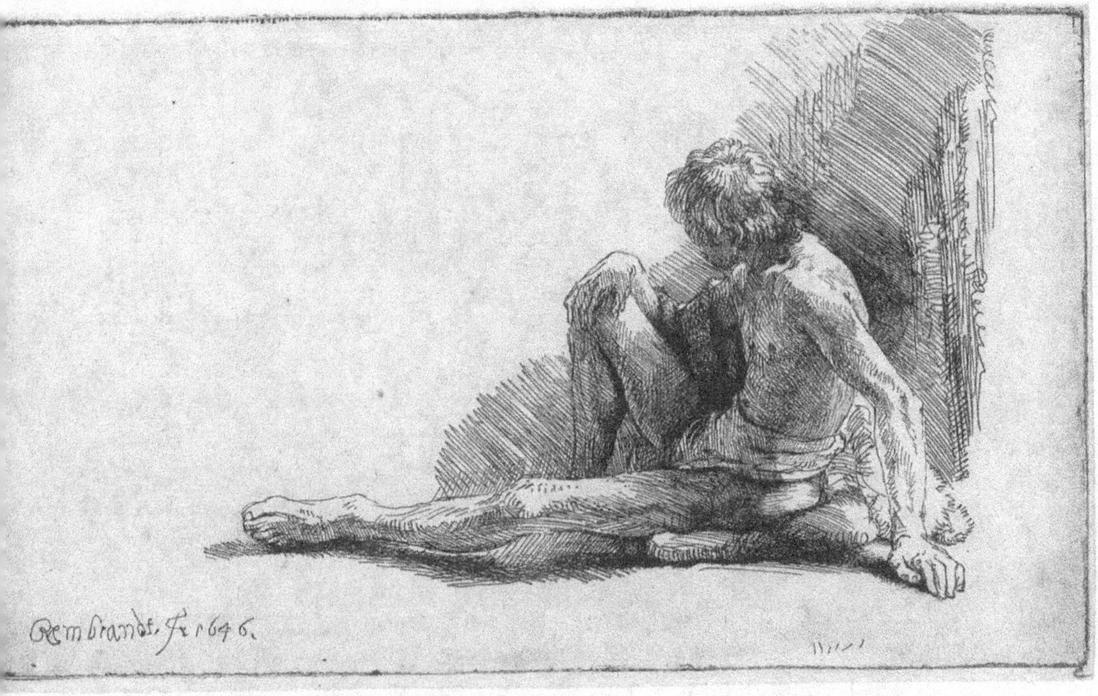

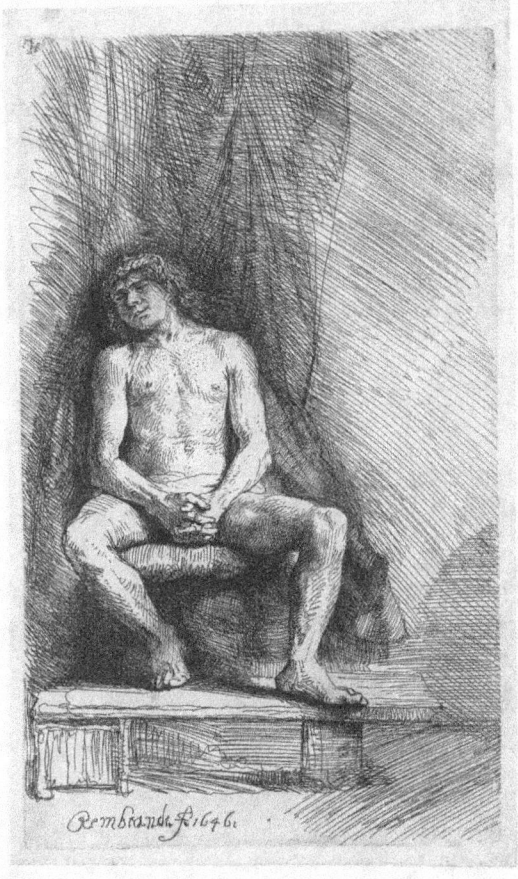

Rembrandt, Nude Man Seated,
1646 (above).
Nude Man Seated Before a Curtain,
Rijksmuseum, Amsterdam (left).

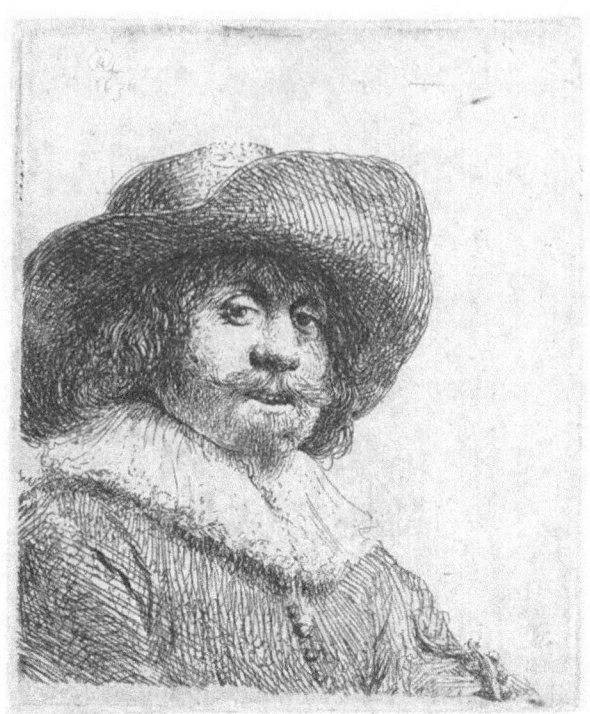

Rembrandt, Man In a Broad-rimmed Hat, 1638 (above).
Man At a Desk, 1641 (below). Both Rijksmuseum, Amsterdam.

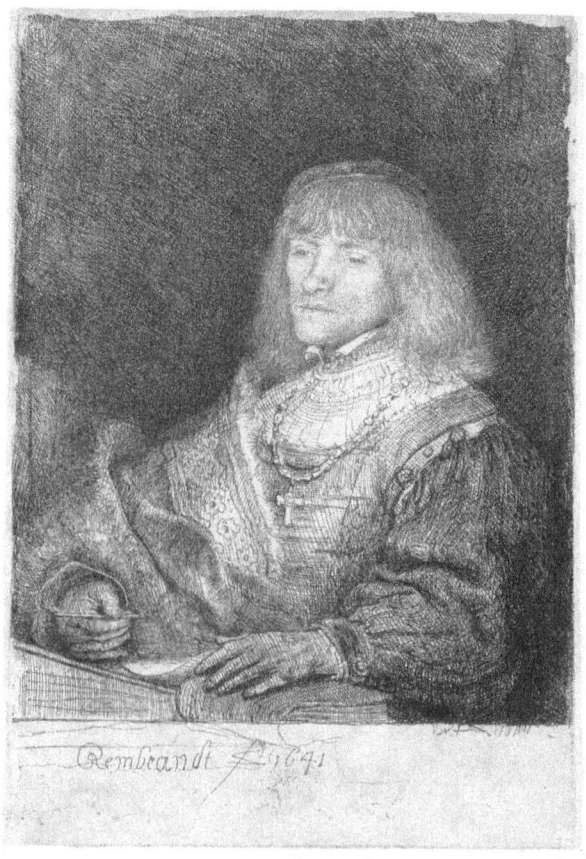

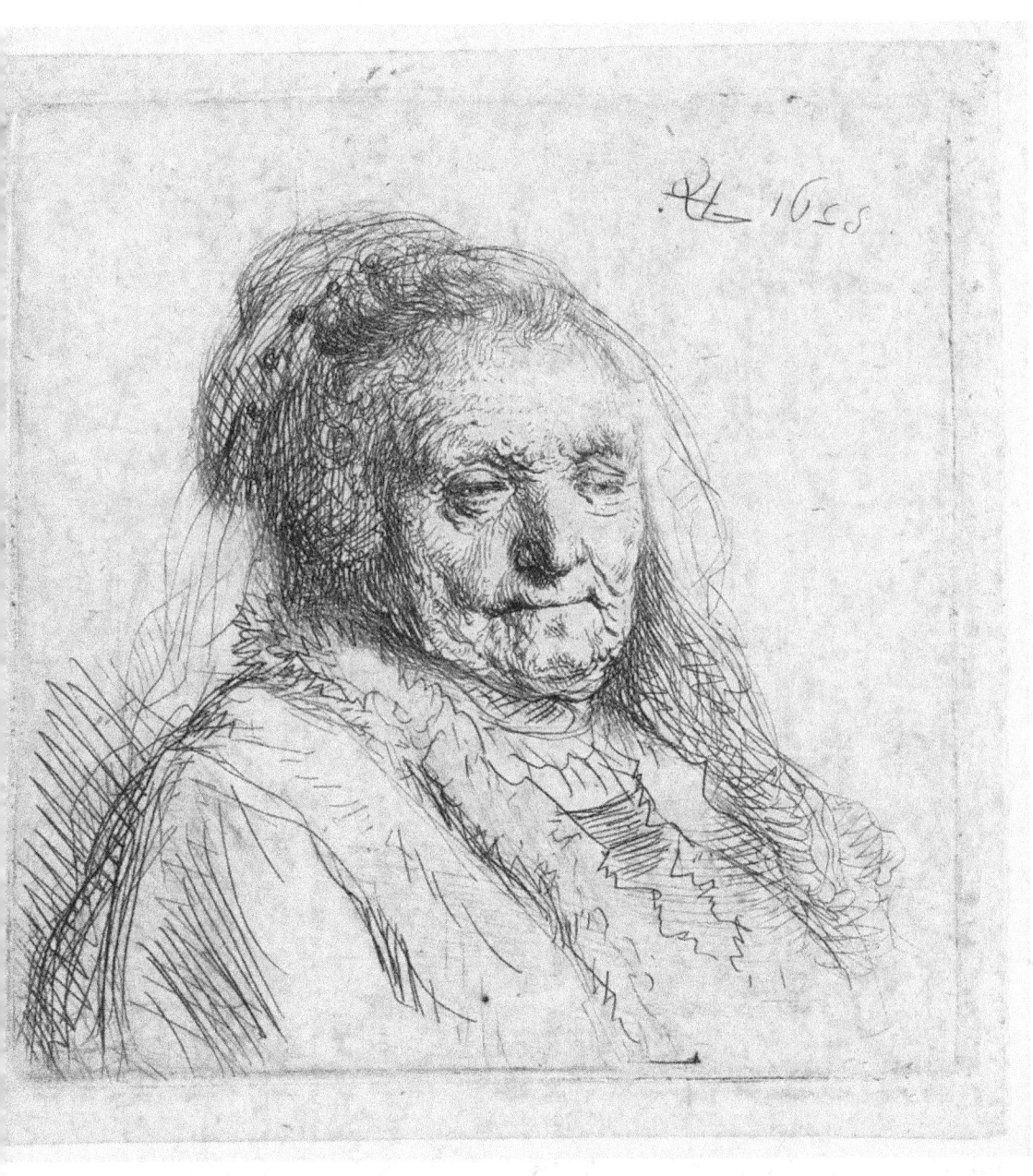

Rembrandt, Mother, 1628, Rijksmuseum, Amsterdam

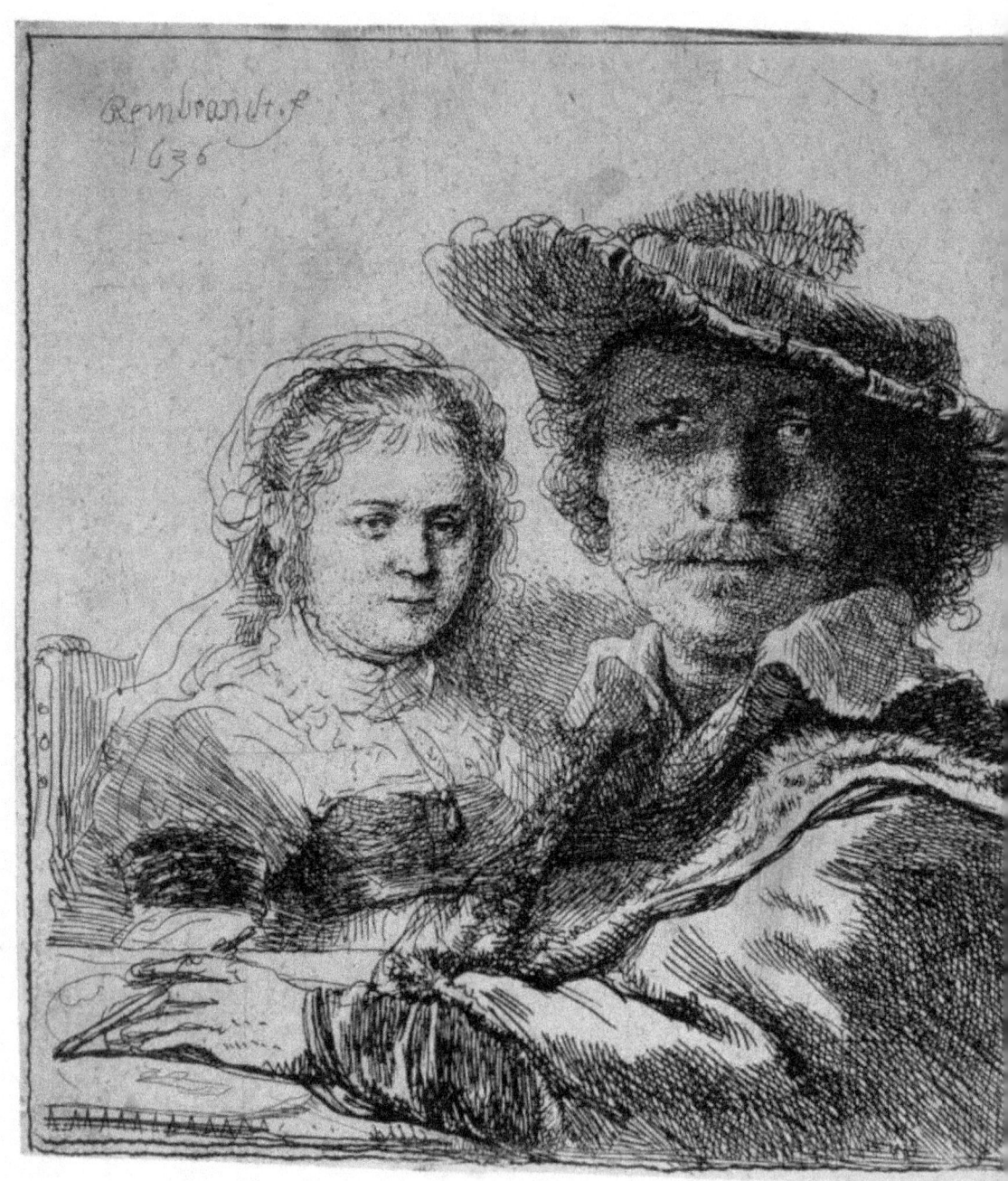

Rembrandt, Self-Portrait With Saskia, 1636, Hermitage Museum

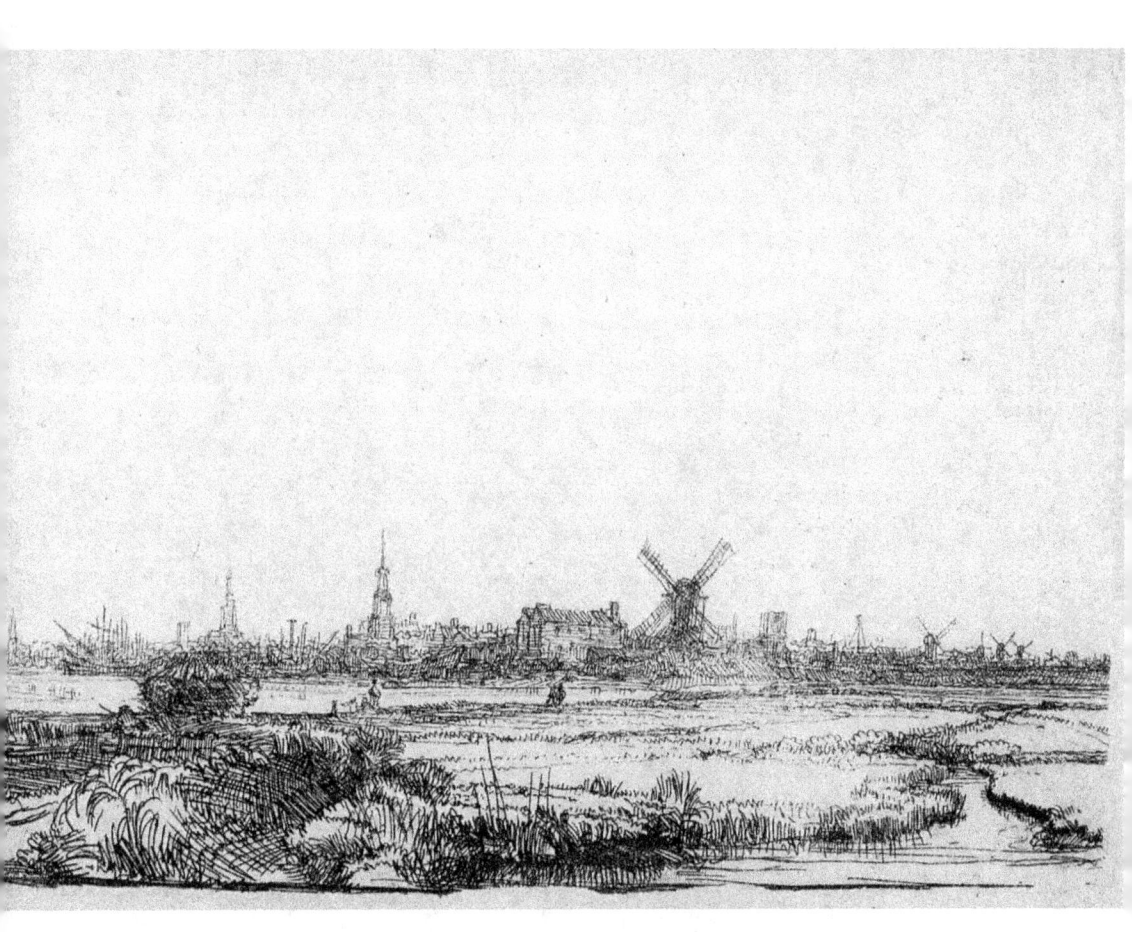

Rembrandt, Amsterdam, c. 1640

CRESCENT MOON PUBLISHING

web: www.crmoon.com e-mail: cresmopub@yahoo.co.uk

ARTS, PAINTING, SCULPTURE

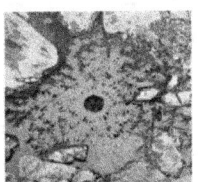

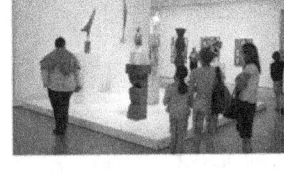

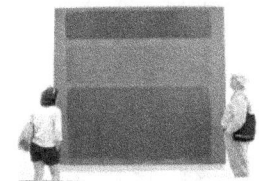

The Art of Andy Goldsworthy
Andy Goldsworthy: Touching Nature
Andy Goldsworthy in Close-Up
Andy Goldsworthy: Pocket Guide
Andy Goldsworthy In America
Land Art: A Complete Guide
The Art of Richard Long
Richard Long: Pocket Guide
Land Art In the UK
Land Art in Close-Up
Land Art In the U.S.A.
Land Art: Pocket Guide
Installation Art in Close-Up
Minimal Art and Artists In the 1960s and After
Colourfield Painting
Land Art DVD, TV documentary
Andy Goldsworthy DVD, TV documentary
The Erotic Object: Sexuality in Sculpture From Prehistory to the Present Day
Sex in Art: Pornography and Pleasure in Painting and Sculpture
Postwar Art
Sacred Gardens: The Garden in Myth, Religion and Art
Glorification: Religious Abstraction in Renaissance and 20th Century Art
Early Netherlandish Painting
Leonardo da Vinci
Piero della Francesca
Giovanni Bellini
Fra Angelico: Art and Religion in the Renaissance
Mark Rothko: The Art of Transcendence
Frank Stella: American Abstract Artist
Jasper Johns
Brice Marden
Alison Wilding: The Embrace of Sculpture
Vincent van Gogh: Visionary Landscapes
Eric Gill: Nuptials of God
Constantin Brancusi: Sculpting the Essence of Things
Max Beckmann
Caravaggio
Gustave Moreau
Egon Schiele: Sex and Death In Purple Stockings
Delizioso Fotografico Fervore: Works In Process 1
Sacro Cuore: Works In Process 2
The Light Eternal: J.M.W. Turner
The Madonna Glorified: Karen Arthurs

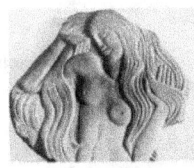

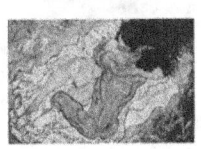

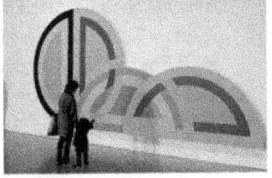

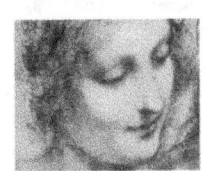

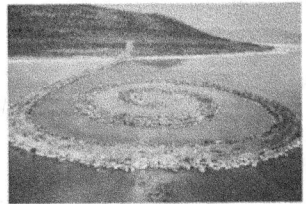

LITERATURE

J.R.R. Tolkien: The Books, The Films, The Whole Cultural Phenomenon
J.R.R. Tolkien: Pocket Guide
Tolkien's Heroic Quest
The *Earthsea* Books of Ursula Le Guin
Beauties, Beasts and Enchantment: Classic French Fairy Tales
German Popular Stories by the Brothers Grimm
Philip Pullman and *His Dark Materials*
Sexing Hardy: Thomas Hardy and Feminism
Thomas Hardy's *Tess of the d'Urbervilles*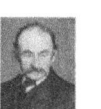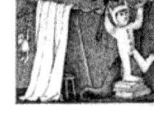
Thomas Hardy's *Jude the Obscure*
Thomas Hardy: The Tragic Novels
Love and Tragedy: Thomas Hardy
The Poetry of Landscape in Hardy
Wessex Revisited: Thomas Hardy and John Cowper Powys
Wolfgang Iser: Essays and Interviews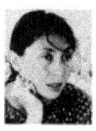
Petrarch, Dante and the Troubadours
Maurice Sendak and the Art of Children's Book Illustration
Andrea Dworkin
Cixous, Irigaray, Kristeva: The *Jouissance* of French Feminism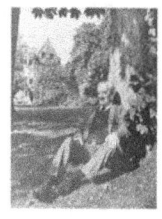
Julia Kristeva: Art, Love, Melancholy, Philosophy, Semiotics and Psychoanalysis
Hélène Cixous I Love You: The *Jouissance* of Writing
Luce Irigaray: Lips, Kissing, and the Politics of Sexual Difference
Peter Redgrove: Here Comes the Flood
Peter Redgrove: Sex-Magic-Poetry-Cornwall
Lawrence Durrell: Between Love and Death, East and West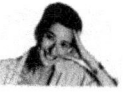
Love, Culture & Poetry: Lawrence Durrell
Cavafy: Anatomy of a Soul
German Romantic Poetry: Goethe, Novalis, Heine, Hölderlin
Feminism and Shakespeare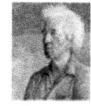
Shakespeare: Love, Poetry & Magic
The Passion of D.H. Lawrence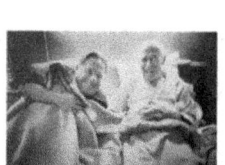
D.H. Lawrence: Symbolic Landscapes
D.H. Lawrence: Infinite Sensual Violence
Rimbaud: Arthur Rimbaud and the Magic of Poetry
The Ecstasies of John Cowper Powys
Sensualism and Mythology: The Wessex Novels of John Cowper Powys
Amorous Life: John Cowper Powys and the Manifestation of Affectivity (H.W. Fawkner)
Postmodern Powys: New Essays on John Cowper Powys (Joe Boulter)
Rethinking Powys: Critical Essays on John Cowper Powys
Paul Bowles & Bernardo Bertolucci
Rainer Maria Rilke
Joseph Conrad: *Heart of Darkness*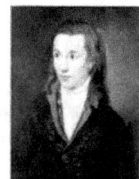
In the Dim Void: Samuel Beckett
Samuel Beckett Goes into the Silence
André Gide: Fiction and Fervour
Jackie Collins and the Blockbuster Novel
Blinded By Her Light: The Love-Poetry of Robert Graves
The Passion of Colours: Travels In Mediterranean Lands
Poetic Forms

POETRY

Ursula Le Guin: Walking In Cornwall
Peter Redgrove: Here Comes The Flood
Peter Redgrove: Sex-Magic-Poetry-Cornwall
Dante: Selections From the Vita Nuova
Petrarch, Dante and the Troubadours
William Shakespeare: Sonnets
William Shakespeare: Complete Poems
Blinded By Her Light: The Love-Poetry of Robert Graves
Emily Dickinson: Selected Poems
Emily Brontë: Poems
Thomas Hardy: Selected Poems
Percy Bysshe Shelley: Poems
John Keats: Selected Poems
Joh n Keats: Poems of 1820
D.H. Lawrence: Selected Poems
Edmund Spenser: Poems
Edmund Spenser: Amoretti
John Donne: Poems
Henry Vaughan: Poems
Sir Thomas Wyatt: Poems
Robert Herrick: Selected Poems
Rilke: Space, Essence and Angels in the Poetry of Rainer Maria Rilke
Rainer Maria Rilke: Selected Poems
Friedrich Hölderlin: Selected Poems
Arseny Tarkovsky: Selected Poems
Arthur Rimbaud: Selected Poems
Arthur Rimbaud: A Season in Hell
Arthur Rimbaud and the Magic of Poetry
Novalis: Hymns To the Night
German Romantic Poetry
Paul Verlaine: Selected Poems
Elizaethan Sonnet Cycles
D.J. Enright: By-Blows
Jeremy Reed: Brigitte's Blue Heart
Jeremy Reed: Claudia Schiffer's Red Shoes
Gorgeous Little Orpheus
Radiance: New Poems
Crescent Moon Book of Nature Poetry
Crescent Moon Book of Love Poetry
Crescent Moon Book of Mystical Poetry
Crescent Moon Book of Elizabethan Love Poetry
Crescent Moon Book of Metaphysical Poetry
Crescent Moon Book of Romantic Poetry
Pagan America: New American Poetry

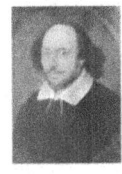
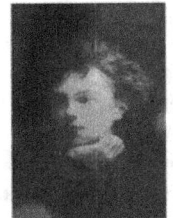
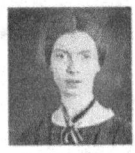
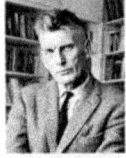
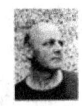
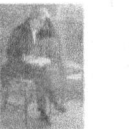
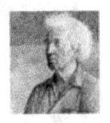
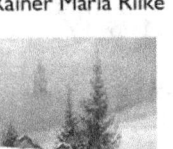
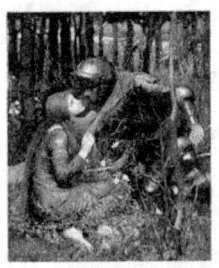
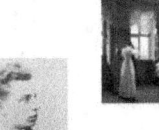
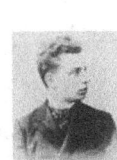
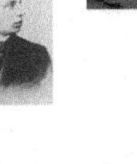
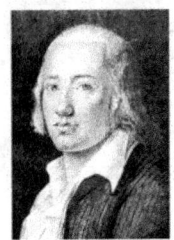
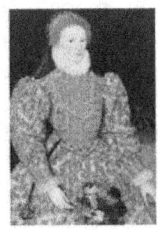

MEDIA, CINEMA, FEMINISM and CULTURAL STUDIES

J.R.R. Tolkien: The Books, The Films, The Whole Cultural Phenomenon
J.R.R. Tolkien: Pocket Guide
The *Lord of the Rings* Movies: Pocket Guide
The Cinema of Hayao Miyazaki
Hayao Miyazaki: *Princess Mononoke*: Pocket Movie Guide
Hayao Miyazaki: *Spirited Away*: Pocket Movie Guide
Tim Burton : Hallowe'en For Hollywood
Ken Russell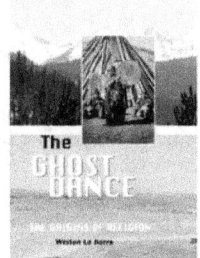
Ken Russell: *Tommy*: Pocket Movie Guide
The Ghost Dance: The Origins of Religion
The Peyote Cult
Cixous, Irigaray, Kristeva: The *Jouissance* of French Feminism
Julia Kristeva: Art, Love, Melancholy, Philosophy, Semiotics and Psychoanalysis
Luce Irigaray: Lips, Kissing, and the Politics of Sexual Difference
Hélene Cixous I Love You: The *Jouissance* of Writing
Andrea Dworkin
'Cosmo Woman': The World of Women's Magazines
Women in Pop Music
HomeGround: The Kate Bush Anthology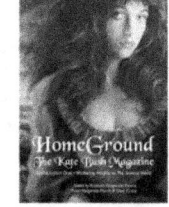
Discovering the Goddess (Geoffrey Ashe)
The Poetry of Cinema
The Sacred Cinema of Andrei Tarkovsky
Andrei Tarkovsky: Pocket Guide
Andrei Tarkovsky: *Mirror*: Pocket Movie Guide
Andrei Tarkovsky: *The Sacrifice*: Pocket Movie Guide
Walerian Borowczyk: Cinema of Erotic Dreams
Jean-Luc Godard: The Passion of Cinema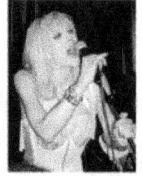
Jean-Luc Godard: *Hail Mary*: Pocket Movie Guide
Jean-Luc Godard: *Contempt*: Pocket Movie Guide
Jean-Luc Godard: *Pierrot le Fou*: Pocket Movie Guide
John Hughes and Eighties Cinema
Ferris Bueller's Day Off: Pocket Movie Guide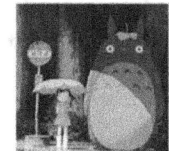
Jean-Luc Godard: Pocket Guide
The Cinema of Richard Linklater
Liv Tyler: Star In Ascendance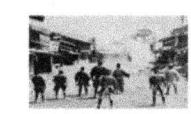
Blade Runner and the Films of Philip K. Dick
Paul Bowles and Bernardo Bertolucci
Media Hell: Radio, TV and the Press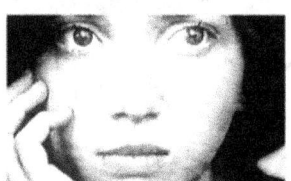
An Open Letter to the BBC
Detonation Britain: Nuclear War in the UK
Feminism and Shakespeare
Wild Zones: Pornography, Art and Feminism
Sex in Art: Pornography and Pleasure in Painting and Sculpture
Sexing Hardy: Thomas Hardy and Feminism

The Light Eternal is a model monograph, an exemplary job. The subject matter of the book is beautifully
organised and dead on beam. (Lawrence Durrell)
It is amazing for me to see my work treated with such passion and respect. (Andrea Dworkin)

CRESCENT MOON PUBLISHING
P.O. Box 1312, Maidstone, Kent, ME14 5XU, Great Britain. www.crmoon.com

cresmopub@yahoo.co.uk   www.crescentmoon.org.uk

www.ingramcontent.com/pod-product-compliance
Lightning Source LLC
Chambersburg PA
CBHW051327220526
45468CB00004B/1537